Charlotte Mason
Study Guide

A Simplified
Approach to a
"Living" Education

Charlotte Mason
Study Guide

A Simplified
Approach to a
"Living" Education

Penny Gardner

Charlotte Mason Study Guide

To obtain additional copies or schedule speaking engagements with the
author please write:

Penny Gardner
PO Box 900983
Sandy, UT 84090-0983
http://members.aol.com/CMSGpenny

Gardner

Layout and Cover by: *SunRise Publishing, Orem, Utah*
ISBN: 1-57636-039-3
Library of Congress Catalog Card Number: 97-67531

Table of Contents

Introduction

This book is based upon the work of Charlotte Mason. It is intended as an aid for those wishing to read her challenging set of book, *The Original Home Education Series*. Quotes (or my paraphrasing) from her books are arranged by topic, followed by study suggestions listing the volumes and chapters which will expand our knowledge of that topic. Articles that may help you apply the topic to your educational endeavors follow some study topics.

The goal of this book is to break down and condense Miss Mason's books into easy to study chunks, making her set less overwhelming and intimidating. This guide is intended as a starting point and an introduction to her profound educational ideas.

So dig in! You may want to set a goal to study one topic a month (if you take a couple of busy months off, this guide will take you two years to get through). Perhaps you have friends who would like to form a study group with you so you can share insights after the month of study and application. Or you may choose to hurry through the entire study guide for a quick overview of the method; then go back to take your time studying more thoroughly, reading the study suggestions as you go.

My thanks go to Karen Andreola, Jean Howery, Donna Goff, and Karen Rackliffe for contributing articles. I would like to also thank Catherine Levison who gave me support through her letters containing encouragement and advice and to my family who supported my efforts. Most especially I'd like to thank Charlotte Mason for showing me a better way to educate my children.

Traveling the Scenic Byway

Some of the roads we travel as we educate our children are arduous, making us weary. Following the Charlotte Mason road is a gentle trip in the English countryside. Miss Mason built this road in 1885 and continued to work on it until her death in 1923. But the road didn't close; others who had experienced this lovely journey continued using and promoting Charlotte Mason's philosophy of education. During the past dozen years, home educators in the United States have discovered this enchanting country lane.

Nature studies, the arts, great literature, building noble characters, and knowing our Lord are some of the materials of its pavement. Miss Mason said, "To form in his child right habits of thinking and behaving is a parent's chief duty.... To nourish a child daily with loving, right, and noble ideas... is the parent's next duty.... The child, having once received the idea, will assimilate it in his own way, and work it into the fabric of his life.... Nourish him with ideas which may bear fruit in his life."

Charlotte Mason wrote *The Original Homeschooling Series*, a six-volume set. But now there is a less time-consuming option. The *Charlotte Mason Study Guide: A Simplified Approach to a "Living" Education* is a condensation of Miss Mason's works. It also contains current writings on how to apply this philosophy in today's home schools. To order, send $9.95 plus $2 shipping to Penny Gardner, PO Box 900983, Sandy, UT 84090.

For now, this is a road less traveled. As the word spreads, it will become a more popular route—though no less pleasant. The *Charlotte Mason Study Guide* is the map to help you find your way as you travel this scenic byway to a great education.

Charlotte Mason: A Woman of Wisdom

Charlotte Mason was a remarkable woman who was ahead of her time and perhaps ahead of our time. She developed a comprehensive and unique way of educating children. She has left many words of wisdom for us in her writings.

Charlotte was born on New Year's Day in 1842 in England. Both her parents were only children, as was Charlotte herself. So Charlotte had no aunts, uncles, cousins, siblings, or even living grandparents. Both her parents died when she was 16 leaving her in poor circumstances.

When she was 18, she attended a teacher's training college. After a year, they let her start teaching because of her financial situation. She received her certificate two years later. She taught at Davidson School in Sussex for a dozen years. But her health was poor and she had to leave her responsibilities.

She wrote some popular geography books about her travels in England. Then in the winter of 1885-86 she gave a series of lectures to raise funds for her church. The lectures were so well received by parents that soon *Home Education* was published from these lectures. She became a busy lecturer.

So many people were expressing interest in her ideas, that in 1887, she started a Parents' Educational Union. *Parents' Review,* a periodical, was started in 1890 as an educational tool to keep parents and teachers on solid footing with the principles that Charlotte was expounding. In 1892 the Parents' National Educational Union and the House of Education (a governess-training college) were established.

By Charlotte's death in 1923, almost every public school in Gloucester County and several other small pockets in Great Britain were using the Mason method. Thousands of children from all classes were benefiting from her gentle educational revolution. Children from the coal mine communities had as rich an education as affluent children.

CHILDREN ARE PERSONS

One of Charlotte's ideas was that children are persons. She treated all persons, whether child or college student or associate—regardless of

class—with courtesy and respect. A student at her college said, "The first thing that struck me was Miss Mason's marvelous courtesy—she knew only the bare outlines of our previous lives, but she spoke to us all as 'persons' and helped us to be dignified by treating us with dignity."

A child, who visited Miss Mason with her mother, years later wrote, "She radiated affection and gaiety... I think children appreciated the serene happiness of her temperament. She never seemed to have 'moods' and although her cares and responsibilities must have been great one never saw her in the least depressed."

Charlotte frequently said, "Always remember that persons matter more than things. Don't say anything that will leave a sting."

MASTERLY INACTIVITY

Another principle, which Charlotte advocated and put into practice herself, was 'masterly inactivity.' This means not stepping in, taking initiative away from the child. Let the child reap the natural consequences of his actions. She said, "We are very tenacious of the dignity and individuality of our children... Do not take too much upon ourselves, but leave time and scope for the workings of Nature and of a higher Power than Nature herself... The art of standing aside to let a child develop the relations proper to him is the fine art of education."

Miss Kitching, who lived and worked with Charlotte Mason for many years wrote, "She never let herself be 'anxious.' She avoided expressions of personal opinion lest they should act like 'suggestion' on those who loved her. She distrusted personal influence as limiting and belittling the person influenced and she steadily set her face against any form of personal influence over any with whom she came in contact. She laid down principles and waited for others to think along her lines of thought and find the right solution. She would not deliver those she loved from the growing pains of thinking for themselves, and sometimes those who did not understand took her silence for consent when they suggested things she did not wish. They little knew that she was only waiting for them to think clearly for themselves.

"Life was too full, she was too frail, it is true, to talk much and also she did not think it wise to do so. She thought and acted and she wished others to think too. Her 'masterly inactivity' was a thing to wonder at when she could so easily have set things, or thought, going in the way that she thought was right. A word from her, beloved as she was, would have done it: but no, her work had to be done with the mind and heart of a person who must not be weakened by personal influence if the work was to be done by a mainspring and not a lever." (*The Story of Charlotte Mason*, p. 65)

BRINGING OUT THE BEST IN OTHERS

One of her first college students said that Miss Mason had an "extra-ordinary power of getting the best out of everybody."

Mr. Household, who was responsible for the spread of this method of education in the Gloucester schools, said, "When she talked with you she brought out the best that was in you, something that you did not know was there. That is a rare gift. The learned and the great are seldom so endowed. We admire them from afar—and remain afar. She caught you up to her level, and for the time you stayed there; and you never quite fell back again. She had given you new light, new power. She expected much of you, more sometimes than you knew that you had in you to give. But as always she was right: you had it and you gave, and of course gained by giving.

"Her power to inspire deep personal affection in the hearts of many who never saw her was remarkable. Though she taught a new thing, a new way, and in teaching had to show the old things and the old ways for what they really are, her criticism left no sting. She could not be anything but generous and the ways of her mind were wide. She did not make you feel small and foolish. You did not bite your lip or flush with vexation. She lifted and inspired. She did not drive; she led and you went with her by happy choice. In any difficulty she always saw the right way. With few words, always perfectly chosen, yet coming naturally without trace of effort, she said what you knew at once to be the right thing, though you had groped long and had not found it. The right thought and the right word were always there." (*The Story of Charlotte Mason*, p. 134-135)

WORDS OF WISDOM

Here are some nuggets of wisdom found in Charlotte Mason's writings.

"Let information hang upon a principle, be inspired by an idea."

"The mind feeds on ideas and therefore children should have a generous curriculum."

"The getting of knowledge and the getting of delight in knowledge are the ends of a child's education."

"Teachers shall teach less and scholars shall learn more."

"A person is not built up from without but from within, that is, he is living and all external educational appliances and activities which are intended to mold his character are decorative and not vital."

"We hold that all education is divine, that every good gift of knowledge and insight comes from above, that the Lord the Holy Spirit is the supreme of mankind, and that the culmination of all education...is that personal knowledge of and intimacy with God in which our being finds its fullest perfection."

"Education, like faith, is the evidence of things not seen... The only fit sustenance for the mind is ideas... Our business is to give children the great ideas of life, of religion, history, science; but it is the *ideas* we must give, clothed upon with facts as they occur, and must leave the child to deal with these as he chooses."

"No intellectual habit is so valuable as that of attention; it is a mere habit but it is also the hall-mark of an educated person."

"The mind is the instrument of one's education; Education does not produce the mind."

A friend of Miss Mason's said, "Without great thoughts there are not great deeds." Charlotte Mason gave much original thought to education and tested her philosophy for years. The method she established had tremendously successful results with children of all classes and with her college students. She was a true woman of wisdom who performed a great deed for the world when she dedicated her life to education. The Lord blessed her to live a long, full

life—despite serious heart problems—to accomplish this work which He had set for her. May we all have the desire to learn more of her teachings and the wisdom to employ them.

A Short Synopsis by Charlotte Mason

The following synopsis of Charlotte Mason's approach to education is part of the preface of each book in the *Home Education Series*. After you have finished this study guide, come back and read this again. It will refresh your understanding of all that you've learned.

1. Children are born *persons*.

2. They are not born either good or bad, but with possibilities for good and evil.

3. The principles of authority on the one hand and obedience on the other, are natural, necessary and fundamental; but—

4. These principles are limited by the respect due to the personality of child, which must not be encroached upon, whether by fear or love, suggestion or influence, or undue play upon any one natural desire.

5. Therefore we are limited to three educational instruments—the atmosphere of environment, the discipline of habit, and the presentation of living ideas.

6. By the saying, EDUCATION IS AN ATMOSPHERE, it is not meant that a child should be isolated in what may be called a "child environment," especially adapted and prepared, but that we should take into account the educational value of his natural home atmosphere, both as regards persons and things, and should let him live freely among his proper conditions. It stultifies a child to bring down his world to the "child's" level.

7. By EDUCATION IS A DISCIPLINE, is meant the discipline of habits formed definitely and thoughtfully, whether habits of mind or body. Physiologists tell us of the adaptation of brain structure to habitual lines of thought—i.e., to our habits.

8. In the saying that EDUCATION IS A LIFE, the need of intellectual and moral as well as of physical sustenance is implied. The mind feeds on ideas, and therefore children should have a generous curriculum.

9. But the mind is not a receptacle into which ideas must be dropped, each idea adding to

an "apperception mass" of its like, the theory upon which the Herbartian doctrine of interest rests.

10. On the contrary, a child's mind is no mere sac to hold ideas; but is rather, if the figure may be allowed, a spiritual *organism,* with an appetite for all knowledge. This is its proper diet, with which it is prepared to deal, and which it can digest and assimilate as the body does foodstuffs.

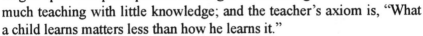

11. This difference is not a verbal quibble. The Herbartian doctrine lays the stress of education—the preparation of knowledge in enticing morsels, presented in due order—upon the teacher. Children taught upon this principle are in danger of receiving much teaching with little knowledge; and the teacher's axiom is, "What a child learns matters less than how he learns it."

12. But, believing that the normal child has powers of mind that fit him to deal with all knowledge proper to him, we must give him a full and generous curriculum; taking care, only, that the knowledge offered to him is vital—that is, that facts are not presented without their informing ideas. Out of this conception comes the principle that,—

13. EDUCATION IS THE SCIENCE OF RELATIONS; that is, that a child has natural relations with a vast number of things and thoughts: so we must train him upon physical exercises, nature, handicrafts, science and art, and upon *many living* books; for we know that our business is, not to teach him all about anything, but to help him to make valid as many as may be of— "Those first-born affinities that fit our new existence to existing things."

14. There are also two secrets of moral and intellectual self-management which should be offered to children; these we may call the Way of the Will and the Way of the Reason.

15. *The Way of the Will.* —Children should be taught—

a) To distinguish between "I want" and "I will."

b) That the way to will effectively is to turn our thoughts from that which we desire but do not will.

c) That the best way to turn our thoughts is to think of or do some quite different thing, entertaining or interesting.

d) That, after a little rest in this way, the will returns to its work with new vigor. (This adjunct of the will is familiar to us as *diversion,* whose office it is to ease us for a time from will effort, that we may "will" again with added power. The use of suggestion—even self-suggestion—as an aid to the will, is to be deprecated, as tending to stultify and stereotype character. It would seem that spontaneity is a condition of development, and that human nature needs the discipline of failure as well as of success.)

16. *The Way of the Reason.* —We should teach children, too, not to "lean" (too confidently) "unto their own understanding," because the function of reason is, to give logical demonstration (a) of mathematical truth; and (b) of an initial idea, accepted by the will. In the former case reason is, perhaps, an infallible guide, but in the second it is not always a safe one; for whether that initial idea be right or wrong, reason will confirm it by irrefragable proofs.

17. Therefore children should be taught, as they become mature enough to understand such teaching, that the chief responsibility which rests on them as persons is the acceptance or rejection of initial ideas. To help them in this choice we should give them principles of conduct and a wide range of the knowledge fitted for them.

These three principles (15, 16, and 17) should save children from some of the loose thinking and heedless action which cause most of us to live at a lower level than we need.

18. We should allow no separation to grow up between the intellectual and "spiritual" life of children; but should teach them that the divine Spirit has constant access to their spirits, and is their continual helper in all the interests, duties and joys of life.

Straight from the Horse's Mouth

During most of Charlotte Mason's life a chief mode of transportation was by horse. Charlotte loved nature. Her daily routine shows what a high priority this was. Charlotte spent nearly two hours outside every afternoon, regardless of the weather or how busy she was. In her younger days, nature walks dominated. But Charlotte's health was never good; this good-hearted woman was victim of a bad heart. So eventually, she had to replace her beloved walks with carriage rides.

Mr. Barrow, who was a gardener and coachman for twenty years at Miss Mason's teacher's college, said: "Miss Mason was fond of her horse, which was a great help in getting close to birds as they don't fear animals so much as persons. And it was always her first inquiry when staying at hotels during Easter holidays —had I and her favorite little mare Duchess been made comfortable and well fed? To her friends who asked why she did not have a motor her answer was: 'I can talk to a horse but not to a motor.' To illustrate her contention that it was so, I very well remember when once by Skelwith Falls on a stormy day Miss Mason wished to return, not feeling well, and she had given me the word to turn again for home. Through the rush of water I had not heard Miss Mason's words, but the Duchess had, and when I attempted to restrain her from turning Miss Mason said it was quite right, Duchess had heard and knew all about it.

"Miss Mason's nerve during these latter years was marvelous, for we encountered all kinds of motorists, reckless and otherwise. We have even had horse's feet on the motor bonnet. Still she kept calm where many a younger person would have been panic-stricken, and probably by leaping out would have caused serious harm to herself.

"Miss Mason was always punctual, never kept man and horse waiting and never left her carriage without the kindly 'Good afternoon' and 'Thank you, Barrow.' And (had our drive been prolific in birds, etc.):

'We've had a splendid bag.'" (from *The Story of Charlotte Mason* by Essex Cholmondeley, p. 67-68)

Charlotte's common sense shows through in her six-volume *Home Education Series.* Here are some quotes illustrating her intimacy with horses.

"You may bring your horse to the water, but you can't make him drink; and you may present ideas of the fittest to the mind of the child; but you do not know in the least which he will take, and which he will reject. And very well for us it is that this safeguard to his individuality is implanted in every child's breast. Our part is to see that his educational *plat* is constantly replenished with fit and inspiring ideas, and then we must needs leave it to the child's own appetite to take which he will have, and as much as he requires." (Vol. 2, p. 127)

"I know you may bring a horse to the water, but you cannot make him drink. What I complain of is that we do not bring our horse to the water. We give him miserable little textbooks, mere compendiums of facts, which he is to learn off and say and produce at an examination; or we give him various knowledge in the form of warm diluents, prepared by his teacher with perhaps some grains of living thought to the gallon. And all the time we have books, books teeming with ideas fresh from the minds of thinkers upon every subject to which we can wish to introduce children." (Vol. 3, p. 170)

"In urging a method of self-education for children...I should like to dwell on the enormous relief to teachers;...the difference is just that between driving a horse that is light and a horse that is heavy in hand; the former covers the ground of his own gay will and the driver goes merrily. The teacher who allows his scholars the freedom of the city of books is at liberty to be their guide, philosopher and friend; and is no longer the mere instrument of forcible intellectual feeding." (Vol. 4, p. 32)

"The children always pay absolute attention, nothing need ever be repeated, no former work is revised; they are always progressing, never retracing their steps, never going round and round like a horse in a mill... Therefore the current textbooks of the schoolroom must needs be scrapped and replaced by *literature,* that is, by books into the writing of which the writer has put his *heart,* as well as a highly trained mind." (*Story of Charlotte Mason,* p. 175, quoted from one of her talks)

There you have it —words of wisdom straight from the horse's mouth. There is much we can learn by studying Charlotte Mason's philosophy and method of education. 'We've a splendid bag' in her timeless ideas which she preserved for us through her writings. May we each have the courage and heart to calmly ride in Miss Mason's carriage in our own hectic day.

Twenty Questions

D o you have questions about the Charlotte Mason philosophy of education? Here are twenty commonly asked questions with brief answers to give you a quick overview.

1. *Who was Charlotte Mason? When did she live?* Charlotte Mason was an innovative educator who developed a unique approach to education. She wanted all children to have a broad, liberal education and to be allowed to reach their full potential. She started a teacher's training college and many parents who educated their children at home flocked to her ideas. Charlotte, a native of England, lived from 1842-1923.

2. *No one I know (including my educator relatives) has heard of Charlotte Mason. Why is this all so obscure?* I've pondered this and come up with the following possible reasons: the Christian viewpoint is now excluded from public schools; Charlotte was a hundred years ahead of her time —most people weren't receptive to treating children and learning as Charlotte advocated; the textbook industry would be non-existent (big business threatened); we don't trust that children are learning unless we see "proof" from standardized testing; schools train for jobs and create mass mediocrity whereas Miss Mason educated in humanities and helped children from all social classes reach their individual potential.

3. *What are the benefits of using her approach?* This is true learning—not superficial. Children's listening, attention, comprehension, retention, speaking and writing skills all improve from using narration as a major part of education. This is an easy, inexpensive way to educate your children.

4. *What exactly is narration?* Charlotte said, "Narration is the mind putting questions to itself." After listening to (or reading for himself) a passage or chapter of a book, the child tells or writes, in his

own words, what he got out of the reading. This requires much more thinking than merely answering someone else's questions.

5. *I'm pleased with our family's approach. Should I add this? And how do I fit it in?* Narration can easily be added to whatever type of home school you have. For those delaying academics, narration is wonderful. You read and listen to your child. You may keep a collection of his oral narrations to show others that he is learning many things. If you are taking a more traditional approach, you are probably requiring writing everyday. Instead of the "What did you do last summer?" sort of writing assignments, let them write meaningfully about the scriptures or the history that they just read. If you do project learning, have them narrate from the resources used.

6. *My kids aren't co-operating. Is this normal? How do I get narrations from them?* Yes, this is normal. Children like to take the easy road; they may not want to add something to the current requirements of your homeschool. Try to make it fun and rewarding. Start with shorter selections; many times you can find something interesting in a single page. Read short, easy chapter books instead of long, challenging ones. Ask for oral narrations even though your older child is capable of writing. Read a book aloud as a family; then while Dad is at work read another chapter that the kids will need to tell Dad about before the next chapter is read to everyone. Put together a collection of narrations as a Christmas gift to relatives. Each child will want to have several of his stories included in this special, joint effort. Let them experience success from the start.

7. *What age should children be when they start narrating?* Charlotte said not to ask a child under six for a narration. However, if your youngster wants to tell you something, listen well. I would not ask written narrations of children until they are at least ten. And then expect a transition period before the child can write a complete narration.

8. *What do I do when my child has mistakes in his written narration?* We don't want to kill the desire to

write by criticizing a child's effort. Sometimes I've volunteered to type the narration, correcting mistakes as I go. Later I can follow up with short lessons on particular problems. One mother has had good results by writing the number of errors at the end of each line. Then the child has the challenge of spotting his mistakes and fixing them. If you have a computer and the child enters the narration, he can use the spell checker himself and eliminate many errors.

9. *What preparation do I need to do?* Narrating is a natural, easy way to learn. It really simplifies home education. You don't need to write lesson plans or research a topic in advance or find 50 enrichment activities to be successful with narration. All you need to do is find a high quality or "living book" which is worth retaining.

10. *What are "living books?"* Charlotte Mason said living books contain living ideas from great minds. Instead of presenting dry facts, these books are written in conversational, literary language. "When a book raises your spirit, and inspires you with noble and manly thoughts, seek for no other test of its excellence. It is good, and made by a good workman," —La Bruyere. "That is a good book which is opened with expectation, and closed with delight and profit," —A. B. Alcott. Many of the classics and Newbery winners (especially the earlier ones) are living books. The King James Version of the Bible is the ultimate living book.

11. *What about math and reading? How did Charlotte Mason say to teach these subjects?* Refer to study guide topic #14 for specifics. One thing Miss Mason said was not to get so hung up on math that there's little time for the humanities; keep math lessons fairly short. Miss Mason felt that many spelling difficulties would be overcome naturally as the child matured and read more. She wrote a grammar book that has a unique slant from the narration angle. It is called *Simply Grammar* and is available from resources listed below in #19.

12. *What subject areas should my children be narrating?* Literature, history, geography, science, Bible study, art appreciation are among the

academic subjects that work really well using a narration approach. Narrations need not be essays. Sketching a map from memory or drawing a diagram of the parts of a flower or listing ten facts that you recall are all valid narrations.

13. *I have children with a wide age span. How do you do narration in a family setting?* One child can tell first with others adding their thoughts when he is through. Sometimes I have just one child narrate from a particular book even though the others are listening. Or an older child can write his narration in another room while mom takes dictation from a younger child. Your child can use a tape recorder to record his narration. An older child can read to a younger child and write down the younger child's narration for him.

14. *What are nature notebooks?* Nature notebooks are a record or journal of the things you observe in nature. They may include watercolors or sketches. The date, common name, scientific name, and the location where observed should all be included. Poetry is a nice touch.

15. *I don't know names of plants, trees, birds, etc. And I'm not artistic. Should we just skip this nature notebook thing?* Nature notebooks are fun. Field guides and other hobbyist are good resources for learning to identify wildlife. It's encouraging to see improvement in art skills as you keep at this new hobby. *Drawing on the Right Side of the Brain* by Betty Edwards uses techniques that have powerful results.

16. *I don't know anything about fine art. Should we still try making an art appreciation notebook?* That's what I like so much about this approach to art appreciation. We don't need to know anything. Let the art speak for itself. We're not teaching our children to be critical of art, but to enjoy it. With just five minutes a week, we can produce a beautiful family keepsake. This is a favorite part of our homeschool. See "Art Appreciation Notebook" in this study guide for a good how-to lesson.

17. *Where do you get the prints for an art appreciation notebook?* Art museums, especially Publications Sales, National Gallery of Art, Washington, D.C. 20565; Art Extension Press, Box 389, Westport, CN 06881; calendars; coffee table books; used books, thrift stores.

18. *I'm confused about all these notebooks. Does each person have their own or do you have one notebook for the whole family?* Each person over six should have their own nature notebook. And each should have their own history notebook and even science notebook, if you choose to keep these. But with the art appreciation notebooks, make just one for the family since it's sometimes difficult and expensive to get art prints. Of course, each individual would contribute narrations and sketches to go with each picture studied.

19. *What resources are there to help me learn more about Charlotte Mason's method?* Your personal library should include these books: *A Charlotte Mason Companion* by Karen Andreola; *A Charlotte Mason Education* by Catherine Levison; *For the Children's Sake* by Susan Schaeffer Macauley; *Educating the WholeHearted Child* by Clay and Sally Clarkson; and this book, *Charlotte Mason Study Guide*. Charlotte Mason's challenging six-volume set is a must for the serious student. If you can't find these resources in your favorite bookstore or catalog, try Charlotte Mason Research and Supply, PO Box 936, Elkton, MD 21922-0936; The Whole Heart Catalogue, PO Box 228, Walnut Springs, TX 76690; or Wholesome Books, 336 E. 1730 S., Orem, UT 84058.

20. *I own Charlotte Mason's set of books. I've started reading the first volume a couple of times but I can't seem to get through it. I'm overwhelmed! What can I do?* We are all overwhelmed by those incredibly profound books. That is the main goal of the *Charlotte Mason Study Guide*—to highlight portions of the original series, arranged by topics, to make studying easier. Then at the end of each study topic, you are referred to corresponding chapters in her series. Our understanding will grow as we study and apply these great precepts.

A Charlotte Mason Education: A How-to Manual

Review of a book by Catherine Levison

Catherine Levison has written a perfect introduction to the Charlotte Mason method. Numerous academic subjects organize this concise, easy-to-read book. Catherine faithfully gives Charlotte Mason's view, then expands the topic with up-to-date ways to apply Miss Mason's philosophy in today's home schools. Lists of living books are included. If you want to quickly grasp and use Charlotte Mason's ideas, this how-to manual will really show you how to. A must.

To order directly, write: Charlotte Mason Communications, 4441 So. Meridian, Suite 221, Puyallup, WA 98373.

Educating the WholeHearted Child A Handbook for Christian Home Education

Review of a book by Clay and Sally Clarkson

The preface to *Educating the WholeHearted Child* declares, "We simply want our children to be wholeheartedly devoted to our God, and to have willing minds that seek and serve him." Clay and Sally Clarkson have pondered deeply to give us fresh insights into true education. Their love for Charlotte Mason's philosophy is wholehearted evident in this practical handbook. (To order directly, see previous page.)

The Child

Charlotte Mason had unique views on the child for her day. The following excerpts from her *Home Education Series* provide an overview of her thoughts on children.

Jesus said to "Take heed that ye OFFEND not —DESPISE not —HINDER not —one of these little ones." (Vol. 1, p. 12)

Don't hinder the child from going unto Jesus. Let him know that he is a beloved child of God. (p. 20)

"A child is a person in whom all possibilities are present —present now at this very moment —not to be educed after years and efforts manifold on the part of the educator." (Vol. 2, p. 260)

"AN ADEQUATE DOCTRINE: The *person* of the child is sacred to us; we do not swamp his individuality in his intelligence, in his conscience, or even in his soul;...or in his physical development. The person is all these and more. We safeguard the initiative of the child and we realize that, in educational work, we must take a back seat; the teacher, even when the teacher is the parent, is not to be too much to the front." (Vol. 3, p. 65)

"CHILDREN AS THEY ARE. —And children have not altered. This is how we find them — with intelligence more acute, logic more keen, observing powers more alert, moral sensibilities more quick, love and faith and hope more abounding; in fact, in all points like as we are, only more so; but absolutely ignorant of the world and its belongings, of us and our ways, and, above all, of how to control and direct and manifest the infinite possibilities with which they are born." (p. 172)

"IS THERE SUCH A THING AS THE 'CHILD-MIND'? —We get courage to attack so wide a program through a few working ideas or principles: one of these is, there is no such thing as the 'child-mind'; we believe that the ignorance of children is illimitable, but that, on the other hand, their intelligence is hardly to be reckoned with by our slower wits. In practical working we find this idea a great power; the teachers do not talk down to the children; they are careful *not* to explain every word that is used, or to ascertain if children understand every detail... In no way is knowledge more enriching than in this of leaving behind it a...dormant appetite for more of the kind... Not what we have learned, but what we are waiting to know, is the delectable part of knowledge. Nor should knowledge be...diluted, but offered to the children with some substance in it and some vitality. We find that children can cover a large and various field with delight and intelligence in the time that is usually wasted over 'the three R's,' object-lessons, and other much-diluted matter in which the teaching is more than the knowledge." (p. 223-224)

STUDY SUGGESTIONS: Vol. 1, Part I, p. 1-41; Vol. 3, Chapter IV, p. 36-43; Vol. 6, Chapter II, p. 33-45

Rights of Children

Charlotte Mason listed SOME OF THE RIGHTS OF CHILDREN AS PERSONS in one of her books. We would do well to keep this list in mind as we interact with our children.

1. "Children should be Free in their Play." Don't crowd out free time or try to structure their play.

2. "Organized Games are not Play." Let children use their own imaginations.

3. "Personal Initiative in Work." Try not to interfere with children at work. They like to decide for themselves to do something and how to do it. Give them time to do their own projects.

4. "Children must Stand or Fall by their own Efforts." Do not prod them. Don't allow children to get in the habit of needing prodding.

5. "Boys and Girls are generally Dutiful. It would be better for boys and girls to suffer the consequences of not doing their work, now and then, than to do it because they are so urged and prodded on all hands that they have no volition in the matter."

6. "Children should Choose their own Friends... We should train children so that we should be able to honor them with a generous confidence; and if we give them such confidence we shall find that they justify it... In this matter, as in all others, the parent's inactivity must be masterly; that is, the young people should read approval or disapproval very easily, and should be able to trace one or the other to general principles of character and conduct..."

7. "Should be free to Spend their own Pocket-Money. In the spending of pocket

money is another opportunity for initiative on the children's part and for self-restraint on that of the parents... The parents who do not trust their young people in this matter, after having trained them, are hardly qualifying them to take their place in a world in which the wise, just, and generous spending of money is a great test of character."

8. "Should form their own Opinions. It is our duty to form opinions carefully, and to hold them tenaciously in so far as the original grounds of our conclusions remain unshaken. But what we have no right to do, is to pass these opinions on to our children." Teach "living principles," not our own opinions.

STUDY SUGGESTIONS: Vol. 3, Chapter IV (p. 36)

Child-Rearing and Discipline

*M*iss Mason had great insight into children and how best to train them. We often tend to ignore what a childless person has to say about parenting. But in this case, these are truly words of wisdom.

The child needs to see that we parents are law-compelled, as is he. Parents *must* not let their child do such-and-such because it is a law of God. Parents cannot be moved or persuaded to change their mind on any question of right and wrong. Parents may offend children by disregarding laws of health, intellect, morality, and need for love. (Vol. 1, p. 15)

"It is as much the parent's duty to educate his child into moral strength and purpose and intellectual activity as it is to feed him and clothe him; and that *in spite of his nature*, if it must be so... The problem before the educator is to give the child control over his own nature, to enable him to hold himself in hand as much in regard to the traits we call good, as to those we call evil." (p. 103)

"The education of habit is successful in so far as it enables the mother to *let her children alone,* not teasing them with perpetual commands and directions; but letting them go their own way and *grow,* having first secured that they will go the right way, and grow to fruitful purpose." (p. 134)

"The mother who takes pains to endow her children with good habits secures for herself smooth and easy days; while she who lets their habits take care of themselves has a weary life of endless friction with the children..." (p. 136)

HABIT OF OBEDIENCE —The parent is "to train the child up to the intelligent obedience of the self-compelling, law-abiding human being." We strive for willing obedience. "The child should be gradually trained in the habit of obedience. His will should be gradually enlisted on the side of sweet service and a free-will offering of submission to the highest law— 'for it is right'." Expect prompt, cheerful obedience. Train the infant to instant obedience. "It is enough to say, 'Do this,' in a quiet, authoritative tone, and *expect it to be done...* The child should be daily confirming a *habit* of obedience by the unbroken repetition of acts of obedience." (p. 161)

"When he is old enough, take the child into confidence; let him know what a noble thing it is to be able to make himself do, in a minute, and brightly, the very thing he would rather not do. To secure this habit of obedience, the mother must exercise great self-restraint; she must never give a command that she does not intend to see carried out to the full. And she must not lay upon her children burdens, grievous to be borne, of command heaped upon command." (p. 164)

"LAW ENSURES LIBERTY. —The children who are trained to perfect obedience may be trusted with a good deal of liberty: they receive a few directions which they know they must not disobey; and for the rest, they are left to learn how to direct their own actions, even at the cost of some small mishaps; and are not pestered with a perpetual fire of 'Do this,' and 'Don't do that!'" (p. 164)

HABIT OF TRUTHFULNESS —There are three causes of lying: carelessness in *ascertaining* the truth, carelessness in *stating* the truth, and a deliberate intention to deceive. Mother should train child to be strictly accurate in all that he says. Allow no exaggeration or embellishment. (p. 166)

Parents as Rulers. Families are absolute monarchies where parents must rule. "The moment [parents] make over [their] functions and authority to another, the rights of parenthood belong to that other, and not to [the parents]." Don't abdicate parental authority by: allowing children "to do what is right in their own eyes"; trying to be popular with our children; giving over their care to someone else; laissez-faire parenting. (Vol. 2, Chap. II)

Limitations and Scope of Parental Authority —Authority is to be exercised solely for the advantage of the children (not for parents' self-interest). Authority is only successful as it encourages the autonomy of the child. We encroach on the child's rights when we make decisions that they are capable of making for themselves. "The highest art lies in ruling without seeming to do so." (p. 17-18)

"Education is a discipline" means education should "deal curatively and methodically with every flaw in character... Discipline is not punishment." Children are our disciples —we lure them to us without using force. Trust "to attraction of the doctrine, to the persuasion of his presentation, to the enthusiasm of his disciples." (p. 66)

The parent should "magnify the quality; make the child feel that he or she has a virtue to guard,...and at the same time a gift from above." If a child has a defect in his character, his mother should devote constant care to him for a month or six weeks. He should always be under a "watchful, loving, and approving eye. Keep him happily occupied." Break his old bad habits with new ones of service, and constructive activities. Replace a bad habit with a new, good one. Don't let bad behavior continue and become a lifetime flaw. (from chapter IX)

Punishment by consequences: "the need for punishment is mostly preventable." Punishments are not "drastic enough to cure the child of the offense. Instead we need to find that weak place in character, [that] false habit of thinking." Deal with this false habit "by forming the contrary habit of true thinking... Not mere spurts of occasional punishment, but the incessant watchfulness and endeavor which go to the forming

and preserving of the habits of the good life, is what we mean by discipline." (p.172) "The well-brought-up child has always been a child carefully trained in good habits." (p. 174)

DOCILITY AND AUTHORITY IN THE HOME AND SCHOOL. Parents are commissioned of God to have authority over their children. They must rule righteously based on true principles — not on own whims (autocracy). "Authority is neither harsh nor indulgent. She is gentle and easy to be entreated in all matter immaterial, just because she is immovable in matter of real importance; for these, there is always a fixed principle ...Nor [does authority] let them off from any plain duty of obedience, courtesy, reverence, or work. Authority is alert; she knows all that is going on and is aware of tendencies... Timely clemency, timely yielding, is a great secret of strong government." When you realize the children were right, "yield the point graciously and send the little rebels away in a glow of love and loyalty." (Vol. 3, p. 17)

Give no offense. You can just give as the reason for all obedience this saying, 'For this is right.' (p. 22)

"Authority is not only a gift, but a grace... Authority is that aspect of love which parents present to their children; parents know it is love, because to them it means continual self-denial, self-repression, self-sacrifice: children recognize it as love, because to them it means quiet rest and gaiety of heart. Perhaps the best aid to the maintenance of authority in the home is for those in authority to ask themselves daily that question which was presumptuously put to our Lord— 'Who gave Thee this authority?'" (p. 24)

Be good-natured in your position of authority. Have confidence in self. Don't be anxious, domineering, interfering, demanding, etc. Have confidence in the children. (p. 29-30)

"The child who is good because he must be so, loses in power of initiative more than he gains in seemly behavior. Every time a child feels that he chooses to obey of his own accord, his power of initiative is strengthened." (p. 31)

"This is the freedom which a child enjoys who has the confidence of his parents as to his comings and goings and childish doings, and who is all the time aware of their authority ...He has liberty, that is, with a sense of *must* behind it to relieve him of that unrest which comes with the constant effort of decision. He is free to do as he ought, but knows quite well in his secret heart that he is not free to do that which ought not. The child who, on the contrary, grows up with no strong sense of authority behind all his actions, but who receives many exhortations to be good and obedient and what not, is aware that he may choose either good or evil, he may obey or not obey, he may tell the truth or tell a lie; and, even when he chooses aright, he does so at the cost of a great deal of nervous wear and tear. His parents have removed from him the support of their authority in the difficult choice of right-doing, and he is left alone to make that most trying of all efforts, the effort of decision... [The child] must be treated with full confidence, and must feel that right-doing is his own free choice, which his parents trust him to make; but he must also be very well aware of the deterrent force in the background, watchful to hinder him when he would do wrong." (p. 31-32)

Have faith that God will help us bring up the children. (p. 35)

"SELF-DISCIPLINE. —The disciple of habit is never complete until it becomes self-discipline in habits." (p. 107)

"LIMITATIONS OF AUTHORITY. —On the other hand, it is well that they should understand the limitations of authority. Even the divine authority does not compete. It indicates the way and protects the wayfarer, and strengthens and directs self-compelling power. It permits a man to make free choice of obedience rather than compels him to obey. In the moral training of children arbitrary action almost always produces revolt. Parents believe that they are doing well to *rule* their households, without considering the pattern, the principles, and the limitations of parental authority." (p. 127-128)

"Duty can exist only as that which we owe. —It is in their early years at home that children should be taught to realize that duty can exist only as that which we owe to God;

that the law of God is exceeding broad and encompasses us as the air we breathe, only more so, for it reaches to our secret thoughts; and this is not a hardship but a delight. That mothers should love their little children and make them happy all day long —this is part of the law of God: that children are glad when they are good, and sad when they are naughty... Mother or teacher cannot give children a better inheritance than the constant sense of being ruled and encompassed by law, and that law is another name for the will of God." (p. 128-129)

"AUTHORITY IN RELIGIOUS EDUCATION. —A child cannot have a lasting sense of duty until he is brought into contact with a supreme Authority, who is the source of law, and the pleasing of whom converts duty into joy." (p. 137)

Consequences—Instead of scolding children, instruct them kindly so they understand the offense and can learn from it. (Vol. 5, Chap. V)

"The arbitrary exercise of authority on the part of the parent...is the real stone of stumbling and rock of offense in the way of many a child." Arbitrary authority may be too strict or too lenient. Arbitrary authority is our love of power showing. We must watch ourselves continually to make sure we don't exercise unrighteous dominion. We must rule with diligence. We should always build up the child's character, avoiding sarcasm, short tempers, or a slap. (p. 70)

With young children, you can change their habits almost without their notice. With the older child, "You can only aid and abet; give the impulse; the training he must do for himself... The child must train himself, and [the parent] must feed him with motives." Discuss the problem with the child but the child must improve himself. (p. 96)

Let the child know that you know his faults and yet are full of love for him, "regarding the hateful faults as alien things to be got rid of, and holding him, in spite of the faults, in close measureless love and confidence... Where parents know this secret of loving, there are no morose boys nor sullen girls." (p. 116)

Parents act consistently and lovingly as God's agents in bringing up their children. Children should respect, honor, and obey their parents.

GRATITUDE TOWARD PARENTS—don't reproach children for not thanking you. Instead, let them know what a pleasure it is to serve them. You'll still bring your actions to their attention, but in a loving way.

KINDNESS AND COURTESY—Let children see your joy when they are kind and courteous to you; let them see your pain when they are not. Let your kids do service for you. (p. 199)

"What [older children need] is, to have their eyes opened that they may see the rights of others as clearly as their own; and their reason cultivated, that they may have power to weigh the one against the other... He must be reached through his affection; the very feelings, which make him offensive when centered upon himself, are beautiful and virtuous when they flow in the channels of justice and benevolence towards others... It rests with the parent to turn the attention from self to other people, and the affections will flow in that direction to which the attention is turned." (p. 206)

"The mother's task in dealing with her growing daughter is one of extreme delicacy. It is only as her daughter's ally and confidante she can be of use to her now. She will keep herself in the background, declining to take the task of self-direction out of her daughter's hands. She will watch for opportunities to give word or look or encouragement to every growing grace. She will deal with failings with a gentle hand... On discovering such fault, the mother will not cover her daughter with shame; the distress she feels she will show, but so that the girl perceives her

mother is sharing her sorrow, and sorrowing for her sake... It is before her own conscience she must stand or fall now." (p. 243)

"But parents...have a delicate task. There must be subjection, but it must be proud, worn as a distinction, an order of merit. Probably the way to secure this is to avoid standing between children and those laws of life and conduct by which we are all ultimately ruled. The higher the authority, the greater distinction in obedience, and children are quick to discriminate between the mere will and pleasure of the arbitrary teacher or parent and the chastened authority of him who is himself under rule... Docility implies equality; there is no great gulf fixed between teacher and taught; both are pursuing the same ends, engaged on the same theme, enriched by mutual interests; and probably the quite delightful pursuit of knowledge affords the only intrinsic liberty for both teacher and taught." (Vol. 6, p. 71)

"The sense of *must* should be present with children; our mistake is to act in such a way that they, only, seem to be law-compelled while their elders do as they please... Two conditions are necessary to secure all proper docility and obedience and, given these two, there is seldom a conflict of wills between teacher and pupils. The conditions are, —the teacher, or other head, may not be arbitrary but must act so evidently as one under authority that the children, quick to discern, see that he too must do the things he ought; and therefore that regulations are not made for his convenience. (I am assuming that everyone entrusted with the bringing up of children recognizes the supreme Authority to Whom we are subject; without this recognition I do not see how it is possible to establish the nice relation which should exist between teacher and taught.) The other condition is that children should have a fine sense of the freedom that comes of knowledge which they are allowed to appropriate as they choose, freely given with little intervention from the teacher. They do choose and are happy in their work." (p. 73-74)

"What is to be said about obedience, to the heads of the house first, to the State, to the Church, and always to the laws of God? Obedience is the test, the sustainer of personality, but it must be the obedience of choice; because choice is laborious, little children must be trained in the obedience of habit; but every gallant boy and girl has learned to *choose* to obey all who are set in authority." (p. 134)

STUDY SUGGESTIONS: Vol. 2, Chapters II, XVI, XIX; Vol. 3, Chapters I, II, III; Vol. 6, Chapter IV

Hints on Child Training

Review of a book by H. Clay Trumbull

I am always reading parenting books. *Hints on Child Training* is an outstanding book. Mr. Trumbull, a prominent Christian author and speaker in the 1800's, wrote this book after raising his own eight children and being a grandfather. He wrote with wisdom and authority. His whole tone was one of common sense, kindness, sympathy, respect, and love. He was an American who lived at about the same time as Charlotte Mason. I was struck by the similarities of their philosophies on child rearing.

Each of the thirty chapters in this book is a treasure-trove of parenting advice. The only hint I have to offer, for those of us wishing to become better parents, is to read and apply *Hints on Child Training*.

Habits and Character

Establishing good habits and virtuous character in our children is a most important priority in child rearing. Charlotte Mason believed that once we get in the habit of training our children to good habits our road would be much easier to travel.

"If the mother settle it in her own mind that the child never does wrong without being aware of his wrong-doing, she will see that he is not too young to have his fault corrected or prevented. Deal with the child on his *first* offense, and a grieved look is enough to convict the little transgressor; but let him go on until a habit of wrong-doing is formed, and the cure is a slow one; then the mother has no chance until she has formed in him a contrary habit of well-doing. To laugh at ugly tempers and let them pass because the child is small, is to sow the wind." (Vol. 1, p. 19)

Habit is ten times as strong as nature. "But habit, to be the lever to lift the child, must work contrary to nature, or at any rate, independently of her." (p. 105)

"Every day, every hour, the parents are either passively or actively forming those habits in their children upon which, more than upon anything else, future character and conduct depend... It is necessary that the mother be always on the alert to nip in the bud the bad habit her children may be in the act of picking up from [others]." (p. 118)

"The effort of decision...is the greatest effort of life; not the doing of the thing, but the making up of one's mind as to which thing to do first... [This] leads to dawdling habits... Dawdling is a habit to be supplanted only by the contrary habit." Rewards or punishments won't help. After a few words showing where this fault may lead, persuade the child to overcome it. Then for 6 weeks, mother makes sure it does not recur. Catch the child's eye expectantly or touch lightly —don't talk about it.

Never lower your standards or slack off. "Prompt action on the child's part should have the reward of absolute leisure." Once the habit is formed, it is very easy for the child to keep it up. (p. 119)

When the child is learning a new habit, but forgets, call his name pleasantly. When he returns say, "I said I should try to remind you." But don't say the thing. Come up with other ways of gently reminding. Never let it slide and never let it cause friction. Mom is a friendly ally to help his bad memory. (p. 123)

Even babies and toddlers should be getting the good habits of obedience, sense of honor, cleanliness, order, neatness, regularity, manners, punctuality, and attention. "The education of habit is successful in so far as it enables the mother to *let her children alone,* not teasing them with perpetual commands and directions; but letting them go their own way and *grow,* having first secured that they will go the right way, and grow to fruitful purpose." (p. 134)

"The mother who takes pains to endow her children with good habits secures for herself smooth and easy days; while she who lets their habits take care of themselves has a weary life of endless friction with the children... The mother devotes herself to the formation of one habit at a time," and to watching "over those already formed." Mother will pick up the habit of training her children in good habits. It will get easier. Some habits children will naturally pick up through our example. Others require training. (p. 136)

HABIT OF PERFECT EXECUTION— "No work should be given to a child that he cannot execute *perfectly,* and then perfection should be required of him as a matter of course... Closely connected with this habit of 'perfect work' is that of finishing whatever is taken in hand. The child should rarely be allowed to set his hand to a new undertaking until the last is finished." (p. 159-160)

The child should be gradually trained in the habit of obedience. Expect prompt, cheerful obedience. Train the infant to instant obedience. "It is enough to say, 'Do this,' in a quiet, authoritative tone, and *expect it to be done...* The child should be daily confirming a *habit* of obedience by the unbroken repetition of acts of obedience." (p. 162-163)

HABIT OF TRUTHFULNESS —There are three causes of lying: carelessness in *ascertaining* the truth, carelessness in *stating* the truth, and a deliberate intention to deceive. Mother should train child to be strictly accurate in all that he says. Allow no exaggeration or embellishment. (p. 166)

HABIT OF SWEET TEMPER —mother should *"change the child's thoughts* before ever the bad temper has had time to develop into conscious feeling, much less act."

HABIT OF PERSONAL INITIATIVE —children should invent their own games and occupations. "[Nature] will prick the brain with problems and the heart with feelings; and the part of mother or teacher in the early years (indeed, all through life) is to sow opportunities, and then to keep in the background, ready with a guiding or restraining hand only when these are badly wanted." (p. 192)

"It rests with the parents of the child to settle for the future man his ways of thinking, behaving, feeling, acting; his disposition, his particular talent; the manner of things upon which his thoughts shall run." (Vol. 2, p. 29)

"As has been well said, 'Sow an act, reap a habit; sow a habit, reap a character; sow a character, reap a destiny.' And a great function of the educator is to secure that acts shall be so regularly, purposefully, and methodically sown that the child shall reap the habits of the good life, in thinking and doing, with the minimum of conscious effort... He has been brought up to be courteous, prompt, punctual, neat, considerate; and he practices these virtues without conscious effort. It is much easier to behave in the way he is used to, than to originate a new line

of conduct... 'Sow a habit, reap a character'; that is, the formation of habits is one of the chief means whereby we modify the original hereditary disposition of the child until it becomes the character of the man." (p. 124)

"We need to find that weak place in character, [that] false habit of thinking." Deal with this false habit "by forming the contrary habit of true thinking... Not mere spurts of occasional punishment, but the incessant watchfulness and endeavor which go to the forming and preserving of the habits of the good life, is what we mean by discipline." (p. 174)

"The well-brought-up child has always been a child carefully trained in good habits." (p.172)

Nagging doesn't work. Instead to correct the bad habit: 1) Remember that the bad habit is set. 2) Stop the habit for six to eight weeks. 3) This time away from the habit is a natural healing time. 4) Introduce a new habit. 5) Make the new habit contrary to the old, bad habit. 6) "Take a moment of happy confidence between parent and child; introduce, by tale or example, the stimulating idea. Get the child's will with you." 7) "Do not tell him to do the new thing, but quietly and cheerfully *see that he does it* on all possible occasions, for weeks if need be, all the time stimulating the new idea, until it takes great hold of the child's imagination." 8) Make sure the old habit never recurs. 9) If it does happen, don't condone it. "Let the punishment, chiefly the sense of your estrangement, be acutely felt." Let him feel ashamed. Teach the child to pray for help but to also try harder... A parent's chief duty is to form in his child right habits of thinking and behaving. (p. 228)

"...A man is what he has made himself by the thoughts which he has allowed himself, the words he has spoken, the deeds he has done." Some good habits: diligence, reverence, gentleness, truthfulness, promptness, courtesy, etc. The most common error people make when trying to establish a good habit is allowing lapses. (p. 234)

"Education is a discipline —that is, the discipline of good habits in which the child is trained." Schoolwork "should afford opportunity for the discipline of many good habits, and should convey to the child such initial ideas of interest in his various studies as to make the pursuit of knowledge on those lines an object in life and a delight to him." (p. 247)

"Every habit we have formed has had its initial idea, and every idea we receive is able to initiate a habit of thought and of action." (Vol. 3, p. 71)

"We know that 'one custom overcometh another,' and that one idea supplants another. We do not give up a child to be selfish, or greedy, or lazy. These are cases for treatment; and a child who has been cured by his mother of some such blemish will not be slow to believe when he grows up in the possibility of reform for others, and in the use of simple, practical means." (p. 86-87)

"Character is the result not merely of the great ideas which are given to us, but of the habits which we labor to form *upon those ideas*. We recognize both principles, and the result is a wide range of possibilities in education, practical methods, and a definite aim. We labor to produce a human being at his best physically, mentally, morally, and spiritually, with the enthusiasms of religion, of the good life, of nature, knowledge, art, and manual work." (p. 99)

"USE OF HABIT IN PHYSICAL TRAINING. —It is well that a child should be taught to keep under his body and bring it into subjection, first, to the authority of his parents and, later, to the authority of his own will; and always, because no less than this is due, to the divine Authority

in whom he has his being. But to bring ourselves under authority at all times would require a constantly repeated effort of thought and will which would make life too laborious. Authority must be sustained by habit." (p. 104)

SELF-RESTRAINT —practice moderation in exercise and food. (p. 105)

SELF-CONTROL —We can handle emergencies if we have self-control (presence of mind). Don't show feelings of impatience, or resentfulness. Ignore annoyances, inconveniences, and discomfort —be cheerful. (p. 106)

"SELF-DISCIPLINE. —The discipline of habit is never complete until it becomes self-discipline in habits." (p. 107)

LOCAL HABITS —Sometimes children show good habits at one house and poor habits in another. Habits are only fully formed when no supervision is necessary. (p. 107)

QUICK PERCEPTION —Noticing details. "Seeing all that is to be seen, hearing all that is to be heard." (p. 109)

"STIMULATING IDEAS. —A habit becomes morally binding in proportion to the inspiring power of the *idea* which underlies it." (p. 110)

"FORTITUDE. —Touch the right spring and children are capable of an amazing amount of steady effort." We should all learn to endure. (p. 110)

"THE HABIT OF SWEET THOUGHTS." Help the child want to have sweet thoughts by some inspiring idea. "Let us keep before the children that it is the manner of thoughts we think which matters; and, in the early days, when a child's face is an open book to his parents, the habit of sweet thoughts must be kept up, and every selfish, resentful, unamiable move-

ment of children's minds observed in the countenance must be changed before consciousness
sets in." (p. 135)

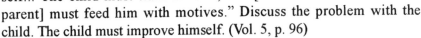

With young children, you can change their
habits almost without their notice. With the
older child, "You can only aid and abet; give
the impulse; the training he must do for himself... The child must train himself, and [the
parent] must feed him with motives." Discuss the problem with the
child. The child must improve himself. (Vol. 5, p. 96)

"Attention is not the only habit that follows due self-education. The
habits of fitting and ready expression, of obedience, of good will, and of
an impersonal outlook are spontaneous by-products of education in this
sort. So, too, are the habits of right thinking and right judging; while
physical habits of neatness and order attend upon the self-respect which
follows an education which respects the personality of children." (Vol. 6,
p. 100)

"There is no other way (than by a course of discipline) of forming
any good habit, though the discipline is usually that of the internal government which the person exercises upon himself; but a certain strenuousness in the formation of good habits is necessary because every such
habit is the result of conflict. The bad habit of the easy life is always
pleasant and persuasive and to be resisted with pain and effort, but with
hope and certainty of success, because in our very structure is the preparation for forming such habits of muscle and mind as we deliberately
propose to ourselves. We entertain the idea which gives birth to the act
and the act repeated again and again becomes the habit; 'Sow an act,' we
are told, 'reap a habit. Sow a habit, reap a character.' But we must go a
step further back, we must sow the idea or notion which makes the act
worth while." (p. 101-102)

STUDY SUGGESTIONS: Vol. 1, Parts III and IV; Vol. 2, VIII, IX, Vol. 5,
Part I

Motto of Education:
"*Education is an atmosphere, a discipline, a life.*"

This motto of education is explained more fully in these quotes. Miss Mason put her sharp mind to work to sum up what education is in these eight words.

"It rests with the parents of the child to settle for the future man his ways of thinking, behaving, feeling, acting; his disposition, his particular talent; the manner of things upon which his thoughts shall run... Education is an atmosphere, a discipline, a life... The Life of the Mind grows upon *Ideas*. Now that life, which we call education, receives only one kind of sustenance; it grows upon *ideas.*" (Vol. 2, p. 29, p. 33)

"What is an idea? A live thing of the mind... We say of an idea that it strikes us, impresses us, seizes us, takes possession of us, rules us... To excite this 'appetency toward something' —towards things lovely, honest, and of good report, is the earliest and most important ministry of the educator." Ideas "are held in that thought-environment which surrounds the child as an atmosphere, which he breathes as his breath of life; and this atmosphere in which the child inspires his unconscious ideas of right living emanates from his parents. Every look of gentleness and tone of reverence, every word of kindness and act of help, passes into the thought-environment, the very atmosphere that the child breathes." (p. 34, p. 36)

"Education is a life; that life is sustained on ideas; ideas are of spiritual origin, and that we get them chiefly as we convey them to one another. The duty of parents is to sustain a child's inner life with ideas as they sustain his body with food." The child will choose this idea or that. (p. 39)

"Education is a discipline" means education should "deal curatively and methodically with every flaw in character... Discipline is not punishment." Children are our disciples—we lure them to us and avoid using force. Trust "to attraction of the doctrine, to the persuasion of his presentation, to the enthusiasm of his disciples." (p. 66)

"Education is a discipline—that is, the discipline of good habits in which the child is trained. Education is a life, nourished upon ideas; and education is an atmosphere—that is, the child breathes the atmosphere emanating from his parents; that of the ideas which rule their own lives." (p. 247)

"We know well that 'Education is an atmosphere, a discipline, a life.' In other words we know that parents and teachers should know how to make sensible use of a child's *circumstances* (atmosphere) to forward his sound education; should train him in the discipline of the *habits* of the good life; and should nourish his life with *ideas,* the food upon which personality waxes strong." (Vol. 3, p. 182)

"Our motto [is], *'Education is an Atmosphere, a Discipline, a Life.'* By this we mean that parents and teachers should know how to make sensible use of a child's circumstances (*atmosphere*), should train him in habits of good living (*discipline*), and should nourish his mind with ideas, the food of the intellectual *life.* These three we believe to be the only instruments of which we may make lawful use in bringing up children... Habits, ideas, and circumstances are external, and we may help each other to get the best that is to be had of them; we may not, however, meddle directly with the personality of child or man." (p. 216-217)

"Education is a life. That life is sustained on ideas. Ideas are of spiritual origin, and God has made us so that we get them chiefly as we convey them to one another, whether by word of mouth, written page, Scripture word, musical symphony; but we must sustain a child's inner life with ideas as we sustain his body with food... He is eclectic; he may choose this or that; our business is to supply him with due abundance and variety and his to take what he needs.... Out of a whole big book a child may not get more than half a dozen of those ideas upon which his spirit thrives; and they come in unexpected places and unrecognized forms..." (Vol. 6, 109)

STUDY SUGGESTIONS: Vol. 2, Chapter IV, VII, XXII; Vol. 6, Chapter VI

Charlotte Mason's Reforms

by Karen Andreola

Education is an atmosphere, a discipline, a life. Motto: "I am, I can, I ought, I will." Education is a life process that is not confined to the classroom. Are we practicing this concept, or are we duplicating the public school classroom regimen in our homes? Are we educating our children for life or for achievement tests?

Whole books and first-hand sources are used whenever possible, *versus* textbooks alone. Facts and information comprise the textbook and are lacking in human emotion. This is deadening to the imagination of the child. Miss Mason advocated what she called "living books."

Children should read the best books, not graded readers or textbook comprehension paragraphs. Educators think they are doing children a favor by taking scissors to cut out pages of the best books. Charlotte called this putting literature in "snippet form." Children deserve to have more than just a nodding acquaintance with the best authors.

A child gains knowledge through his own digging out of facts and information clothed in literary (conversational) language by the use of narration. Miss Mason said that the use of narration is the best way to acquire knowledge from books. Because narration takes the place of the questionnaire, multiple choice, true and false, it enables the child to bring all the faculties of mind into play. With the help of the vocabulary and descriptive power of good writers, the child tells back his own version. Education is for the individual.

There is no need for homework in elementary years because the child immediately deals with the literature at hand. Miss Mason's schools never gave homework? Correct. This allowed for a cozy evening with a good book and parental attention. Education is an atmosphere. Why do Christian private schools bow down to the American homework grind?

The child is introduced to the humanities while he is still young, while he is forming his personality. Education of the person of the child over and above the need for making a living. Short goody-goody

stories are shunned for whole books that follow the life of an admirable character. Morals are painted for the child, not pointed at the child.

We live by admiration, faith, and love *versus* artificial stimulants like prizes, competition and grades. What, there were no grades in her elementary schools? Correct again.

Lessons end at 1:00 PM, and the afternoon is free for leisure. Leisure for children usually means running, climbing, yelling, etc. out of doors. Handicrafts or practice of an instrument, chores, visiting lonely neighbors, nature observation, cooking, may also be accomplished. Unfortunately, public school children arrive home just in time to see the sunset and do homework. What a waste of time and ability! What drudgery!

Through Charlotte's method a child gains the skill to be self-educated. Education is a discipline. There is no dependence upon notes taken of a teacher's lecture where the teacher has predigested most of the information. With Charlotte's method the carefully chosen words of an author are commented on by the child in essay form, either oral or written, starting at age six to seven. Much explaining by the teacher (that includes you, Mom) is a bore. Why is this lecture method still being carried out in high schools?

Inspiring the love of knowledge in children depends on the presentation of ideas. Ideas are what the mind feeds on. To quote Miss Mason, "Ideas must reach us directly from the mind of the thinker, and it is chiefly by the means of the books they have written that we get in touch with the best minds." This includes all forms of human expression. This is why Charlotte said, "Varied humane reading as well as the appreciation of the humanities is not a luxury, a tid-bit, to be given to children now and then, but their very bread of life."

Homeschoolers following Charlotte's philosophy and method try to give their children abundant portions of the humanities at regular periods. They don't allow themselves to get stuck in a routine that emphasizes skills alone. *"Oh, we only had time for math drill, spelling, and grammar, and a few pages from our history textbook today. Tomorrow we will hopefully have time for poetry, and*

maybe a little music appreciation." When fear of a poor showing on the achievement test allows skills to take precedence, humanities take a back seat. The result: lessons become wearisome, children become fed-up, mom gets burned out. The children are starving for knowledge touched with emotion, and for ideas.

Lessons are kept short, enabling children to develop the habit of attention, preventing the contrary habit of dawdling over lessons. *"Oh, you're not finished with your one math page yet? Well, then there is no time for a short romp in the backyard. Perhaps you can finish your math page in less than 15 minutes tomorrow."*

Charlotte didn't concern herself with grammar lessons until the children were well into the habit of narration. It is more important that the child learn to express himself correctly. He should have daily opportunities to have an opinion, make a judgment, no matter how crude, develop a train of thought, and use his imagination. Are you using grammar lessons for first, second, or third grade children that replace this free use of expression? I am disturbed at curricula that claim to be based on Charlotte's method, yet spend time inappropriately breaking down parts of speech to the exclusion of familiarity with the literary content. Let's be careful not to prune the child's natural inclination toward language. In the early years he might score slightly lower on achievement tests, but you can't serve two masters. I have notebooks I've filled with my children's narrations.

When Charlotte said education is a discipline what she meant, in Victorian-day terms, was the wise use of habit. The mother who takes pains to endow her children with good habits secures for herself smooth and easy days. On the other hand, she who lets habits take care of themselves has a weary life of endless friction. The mother needs to acquire her own habit of training her children so that, by and by, it is not troublesome to her, but a pleasure. She devotes herself to the formation of one habit in her children at a time, doing no more than watch over those already formed. Remember, to instill habits:

—Be faithfully consistent. The danger is when we let things go "just this once."

—Forming a habit is using perseverance to work against a contrary habit.

—Formation is easier than reformation. Nip the weed in the bud.

In Charlotte's schools, teachers used different books from year to year. This was intentional. It kept the teachers challenged and supplied with fresh ideas. What are the symptoms of an unsatisfied curiosity in either teacher or student? Simply this, *"Do we have to do school?"* Why not follow Charlotte's advice?

—Whole books; very few textbooks, if any.

—Narration in place of workbooks; grammar is saved for a little later.

—The presentation of ideas; getting in touch with the best minds.

—An emphasis on the humanities; short lessons, especially for drills and skills.

—Formation of good habits.

—Free afternoons; no homework, no grades.

—Unedited literature; no readers.

I'm sure I could add more to the list, but space does not permit. I hope my hodge-podge of notes has given you a peek into one woman's life work.

For a preview issue of *The Parents' Review,* the quarterly magazine published by The Charlotte Mason Research and Supply Co., send $5.00 to:

Charlotte Mason Research & Supply Co.
PO Box 936
Elkton, MD 21922-0936

Ideas, the Sustenance of Life

This topic is so exciting and profound! Charlotte Mason put forth the notion that we should inspire children with the great idea behind a subject or behind a virtue. This puts education in a new light. Her enthusiasm for this concept of ideas is catching.

"What is an idea? A live thing of the mind... We say of an idea that it strikes us, impresses us, seizes us, takes possession of us, rules us... To excite this 'appetency toward something —towards things lovely, honest, and of good report, is the earliest and most important ministry of the educator... Ideas are held in that thought-environment which surrounds the child as an atmosphere, which he breathes as his breath of life; and this atmosphere in which the child inspires his unconscious ideas of right living emanates from his parents..." (Vol. 2, p. 34, 36)

"Education is a life; that life is sustained on ideas; ideas are of spiritual origin, and that we get them chiefly as we convey them to one another. The duty of parents is to sustain a child's inner life with ideas as they sustain his body with food." (p. 39)

When we see a potential talent or gift in the child, we need to provide these four things: "nourishment, exercise, change, and rest."

Exercise: let him use his gift and learn more. Nourishment: "Let him do just so much as he takes to of his own accord; but never urge, never applaud, never show him off... Next, let words convey ideas as he is able to bear them... It is a great thing that the child should get the *ideas* proper to the qualities inherent in him. An idea fitly put is taken in without effort, and, once in, ideas behave like living creatures —they feed, grow, and multiply." Change: "Next, provide him with some delightful change of thought, that is, with work and ideas altogether apart from" his gift. Get intimate with nature or work with clay, wood, paints, etc. Rest: Children should be able to play, rest, daydream, and just relax. This seems to suggest balance in life to me. (p. 76)

"You may bring your horse to the water, but you can't make him drink; and you may present ideas of the fittest to the mind of the child; but you do not know in the least which he will take, and which he will reject... Our part is to see that his educational *plat* is constantly replenished with fit and inspiring ideas, and then we must needs leave it to the child's own appetite to take which he will have, and as much as he requires." (p. 127)

"Next duty is to nourish the child daily with loving, right, and noble ideas. The child having once received the idea will assimilate it in his own way, and work it into the fabric of his life... Nourish him with ideas which may bear fruit in his life." (p. 228)

The study of something is worthwhile if a fruitful idea underlies it. (p. 230)

"All the great ideas that have moved the world" are in books. Don't get between the book and the child. Don't water it down —let the child's mind deal with the matter as it can. (p. 231)

Schoolwork "should convey to the child such initial ideas of interest in his various studies as to make the pursuit of knowledge on those lines an object in life and a delight to him." (p. 247)

"The Great Recognition [is] that God...is the Imparter of knowledge, the Instructor of youth, the Inspirer of genius... But the Florentine mind of the Middle Ages went further than this: it believed, not only that the seven Liberal Arts were fully under the direct outpouring of the Holy Ghost but that every fruitful idea, every original conception, whether in Euclid, or grammar, or music, was a direct inspiration from the Holy Spirit." (p. 270-271)

"A first condition of this vitalizing teaching is that all the thought we offer to our children shall be *living* thought;...given the vitalizing ideas, children will readily hang the mere facts upon the idea as upon a peg capable of sustaining all that is needful to retain." (p. 277)

"Let us say with Plato that an idea is an entity, a live thing of the mind." (Vol. 3, p. 69)

"Every habit we have formed has had its initial idea, and every idea we receive is able to initiate a habit of thought and of action. Every human being has the power of communicating notions to other human beings; and, after he is dead, this power survives him in the work he has done and the words he has said. How illimitable is life!... Every relation must be initiated by its own 'captain' idea, sustained upon fitting ideas; and wrought into the material substance of the *person* by its proper habits. This is the field before us." (p. 71)

"THE AWAKENING IDEA. —It rests with us to give the awakening idea and then to form the habit of thought and of life." A person's great life work might come from a chance conversation that awakens an idea. (p. 81)

"STIMULATING IDEAS. —A habit becomes morally binding in proportion to the inspiring power of the idea which underlies it." (p. 110)

SERVICE, COURAGE, PRUDENCE, CHASTITY. Use heroic examples of these qualities. "Parents would do well to see to it that they turn out their children fit for service, not only by observing the necessary hygienic conditions, but by bringing their bodies under rule, training them in habits and inspiring them with the ideas of knightly service." (p. 111-112)

"Nothing is so practical as a great idea, because nothing produces such an abundant outcome of practical effort." Living ideas, living literature are necessary. (p. 118)

"PLATO'S EDUCATION AIM. — 'He desired not to assist in storing the passive mind with the various sorts of knowledge most in request, as if the human soul were a mere repository or banqueting room, but to place it in such relations of circumstance as should gradually excite its vegetating and germination powers to produce new fruits of thought, new conceptions and imaginations and ideas.'" (p. 125)

"INSPIRING IDEAS OF THE RELIGIOUS LIFE. —The most important part of our subject remains to be considered —the inspiring ideas we propose to give children in the things of the divine life. This is a matter we are a little apt to leave to chance; but when we consider the vitalizing power of an idea, and how a single great idea changes the current of a life, it becomes us to consider very carefully what ideas of the things of God we may most fitly offer children, and how these may be most invitingly presented." (p. 144)

"A man becomes great upon one diet only, the diet of great ideas communicated to those already prepared to receive them by a higher Power than Nature herself." (p. 156)

"WE MAY NOT CHOOSE OR REJECT SUBJECTS. —You will see at a glance, with this Captain Idea of establishing relationships as a guide, the unwisdom of choosing or rejecting this or that subject, as being more or less useful or necessary in view of a child's future... Of course it is only now and then that a notion catches the small boy, but when it does catch, it works wonders, and does more for his education than years of grind.

"Let us try, however imperfectly, to make education a science of relationships —in other words, try in one subject or another to let the children work upon living ideas. In this field small efforts are honored with great rewards, and we perceive that the education we are giving exceeds all that we intended or imagined." (p. 162-163)

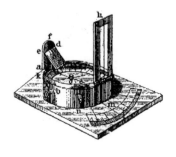

"Living ideas can be derived only from living minds, and so it occasionally happens that a vital spark is flashed from teacher to pupil. But this occurs only when the subject is one to which the teacher has given *original* thought." (p. 169)

"OUR WORK, TO GIVE VITALIZING IDEAS. —Knowing that the brain is the physical seat of habit and that conduct and character, alike, are the outcome of the habits we allow; knowing, too, that an inspiring idea initiates a new habit of thought, and hence, a new habit of life; we perceive that the great work of education is to inspire children with vitalizing ideas as to every relation of life, every department of knowledge, every subject of thought; and to give deliberate care to the formation of those habits of the good life which are the outcome of vitalizing ideas. In this great work we seek and assuredly find the cooperation of the Divine Spirit, whom we recognize, in a sense rather new to modern thought, as the supreme Educator of mankind in things that have been called secular, fully as much as in those that have been called sacred." (p. 172-173)

"We ask ourselves — 'Is there any fruitful *idea* underlying this or that study that the children are engaged in?'...A 'subject' which does not rise out of some great thought of life we usually reject as not nourishing, not fruitful." (p. 174)

"PRINCIPLES ON WHICH TO SELECT SCHOOL-BOOKS.— ...I venture to propose one or two principles in the matter of schoolbooks, and shall leave the far more difficult part, the application of those principles, to the reader. For example, I think we owe it to children to let them dig their knowledge, of whatever subject, for themselves out of the fit book; and this for two reasons: What a child digs for is his own possession; what is poured into his ear...floats out as lightly as it came in, and is rarely assimilated... Ideas must reach us directly from the mind of the thinker, and it is chiefly by means of the books they have written that we get into touch with the best minds." (p. 177)

"HOW TO USE THE RIGHT BOOKS. —The children must enjoy the book. The ideas it holds must each make that sudden, delightful impact upon their minds, must cause that intellectual stir, which mark inception of an idea. The teacher's part in this regard is to see and feel for himself, and then to rouse his pupils by an appreciative look or word; but to beware how he deadens the impression by a flood of talk." (p. 178)

"CHILDREN MUST LABOR. —This, of getting ideas out of them, is by no means all we must do with books. 'In all labor there is profit,' at any rate in some labor; and the labor of thought is what his book must induce in the child. He must generalize, classify, infer, judge, visualize, discriminate, labor in one way or another, with that capable mind of his, until the substance of his book is assimilated or rejected, according as he shall determine; for the determination rests with him and not with his teacher." (p. 179)

Thomas Godolphin Rooper was a member of PNUE and an admired friend of Charlotte Mason. He said, "Without great thoughts there are not great deeds." (Vol. 5, p. 421)

"Mind appeals to mind and thought begets thought and that is how we become educated. For this reason we owe it to every child to put him in communication with great minds that he may get at great thoughts; with the minds, that is, of those who have left us great works; and the only vital method of education appears to be that children should read worthy books, many worthy books." (Vol. 6, p. 12)

"The mind...is nourished upon ideas and absorbs facts only as these are connected with the living ideas upon which they hang. Children educated upon some such lines as these respond in a surprising way, developing capacity, character, countenance, initiative and a sense of responsibility. They are, in fact, even as children, good and thoughtful citizens." (p. 20)

"The life of the mind is sustained upon ideas; there is no intellectual vitality in the mind to which ideas are not presented several times, say, every day." (p. 25)

"Let information hang upon a principle, be inspired by an idea." (p. 26)

"Once we realize that the mind too works only as it is fed, education will appear to us in a new light... For the mind is capable of dealing with only one kind of food; it lives, grows and is nourished upon ideas only; [not] mere information...

"What is an idea? we ask, and find ourselves plunged beyond our depth. A live thing of the mind, seems to be the conclusion of our greatest thinkers... We all know how an idea *'strikes,' 'seizes,' 'catches hold of,' 'impresses'* us and at last, if it be big enough, *'possesses'* us; in a word, behaves like an entity.

"If we inquire into any person's habits of life, mental preoccupation, devotion to a cause or pursuit, he will usually tell us that such and such *an idea struck him.* This potency of an idea is matter of common recognition. No phrase is more common and more promising than, 'I have an idea'; we rise to such an opening as trout to a well-chosen fly. There is but one sphere in which the word idea never occurs, in which the conception of an idea is curiously absent, and that sphere is education! Look at any publisher's list of school books and you shall find that the books recommended are carefully desiccated, drained of the least suspicion of an idea, reduced to the driest statements of fact." (p. 105)

"These indefinite ideas which express themselves in an 'appetency' towards something and which should draw a child towards things honest, lovely and of good report, are not to be offered of set purpose or at set times: they are held in that thought-atmosphere which surrounds him, breathed as his breath of life." (p. 107)

"Education is a life. That life is sustained on ideas. Ideas are of spiritual origin, and God has made us so that we get them chiefly as we convey them to one another, whether by word of mouth, written page, Scripture word, musical symphony; but we must sustain a child's inner life with ideas as we sustain his body with food... He is eclectic; he may choose this or that; our business is to supply him with due abundance and variety and his to take what he needs... Out of a whole big book a child may not get more than half a dozen of those ideas upon which his spirit thrives; and they come in unexpected places and unrecognized forms, so that no grown person is capable of making such extracts from Scott or Dickens or Milton, as will certainly give him nourishment. It is a case of, — 'In the morning sow thy seed and in the evening withhold not thine hand for thou knowest not whether shall prosper, either this or that.'

"One of our presumptuous sins in this connection is that we venture to offer opinions to children (and to older persons) instead of ideas. We believe that an opinion expresses thought and therefore embodies an idea. Even if it did so, once the very act of crystallization into opinion destroys any vitality it may have had." (p. 109-110)

"All roads lead to Rome, and all I have said is meant to enforce the fact that much and varied humane reading, as well as human thought expressed in the forms of art, is, not luxury, a tid-bit, to be given to children now and then, but their very bread of life, which they must have in abundant portions and at regular periods. This and more is implied in the phrase, 'The mind feeds on ideas and therefore children should have a generous curriculum.'" (p. 111)

"This is the way to make great men and not by petty efforts to form character in this direction or in that. Let us take it to ourselves that great character comes out of great thoughts, and that great thought must be initiated by great thinkers; then we shall have a definite aim in education." (p. 278)

STUDY SUGGESTIONS: Vol. 1, Part V, Chapter I; Vol. 2, Chapter IV; Vol. 6, Introduction, Chapter I, part of Chapter IV (p. 104-111), and optional—Chapter VII.

Education is the Science of Relations

*A*s parents we want our children to relate to the world around them. We want them to come face to face with greatness—to be inspired by some of the incredible people who have enriched our lives. We want them to live rich, full lives.

"EDUCATION THE SCIENCE OF RELATIONS. —We consider that *education is the science of relations*, or, more fully, that education considers what relations are proper to a human being, and in what ways these several relations can best be established; that a human being comes into the world with capacity for many relations; and that we, for our part, have two chief concerns —first, to put him in the way of forming these relations by presenting the right idea at the right time, and by forming the right habit upon the right idea; and, secondly, by not getting in the way and so preventing the establishment of the very relations we seek to form." (Vol. 3, p. 65-66)

TEACHING MUST NOT BE OBTRUSIVE. Avoid lectures. Personally know objects, or nature. Form relationships with actual things. We want the child to establish "relations with great minds and various minds." Don't get between child and great minds. (p. 66)

"THE ART OF STANDING ASIDE. —The art of standing aside to let a child develop the relations proper to him is the fine art of education." (p. 66-67)

"The very word education is a misnomer... We shall have some fit new word meaning, perhaps, 'applied wisdom,' for wisdom is *the science of relations*, and the thing we have to do for a young human being is to put him in touch, so far as we can, with all the relations proper to him... Fullness of living, joy in life, depend, far more than we know,

upon the establishment of these relations." (p. 75)

"THE POWER OF RECOGNITION. —His parents know that the first step in intimacy is recognition; and they will measure his education, not solely by his progress in the 'three R's,' but by the number of living and growing things he knows by look, name, and habitat." (p. 76)

"APPRECIATIVE KNOWLEDGE AND EXACT KNOWLEDGE. —All the time he is storing up associations of delight which will come back for his refreshment when he is an old man. With this sort of appreciative knowledge of things to begin with, the superstructure of exact knowledge, living science, no mere affair of text-books and examinations, is easily raised, because a natural desire is implanted." (p. 77-78)

"HOW A CHILD SETS UP A NEW RELATION. —The setting up of relations, moral and intellectual, is our chief concern in life, and that the function of education is to put the child in the way of relations proper to him, and to offer the inspiring idea which commonly initiates a relation." (p. 78)

CERTAIN RELATIONS PROPER TO A CHILD —Children should gather common information about our world (the sciences). Children need to know how to run, jump, skate, swim, dance, row a boat, and more. They should delight in making things with their hands from mud-pies and sandcastles to sewing and woodworking. They should have relations with animals. (from Chapter VIII)

"THE GREAT HUMAN RELATIONSHIPS. —Perhaps the main part of a child's education should be concerned with the great human relationships, relationships of love and service, of authority and obedience, of

reverence and pity and neighborly kindness; relationships to kin and friend and neighbor, to 'cause' and country and kind, to the past and the present. History, literature, archaeology, art, languages, whether ancient or modern, travel and tales of travel; all of these are in one way or other the record or the expression of persons." (p. 80)

"HUMAN INTELLIGENCE LIMITED TO HUMAN INTERESTS.—...*The limit to human intelligence arises largely from the limit to human interests,* that is, from the failure to establish personal relations on a wide scale with the persons who make up humanity, —relations of love, duty, responsibil-  ity, and, above all, of interest, *living* interest, with the near and the far-off, in time and in place." (p. 82)

"THE FULL HUMAN LIFE. —I think we should have a great educational revolution once we...realized ourselves as persons whose great business it is to get in touch with other persons of all sorts and conditions, of all countries and climes, of all times, past and present. History would become entrancing, literature, a magic mirror for the discovery of other minds, the study of sociology, a duty and a delight. We should tend to become responsive and wise, humble and reverent, recognizing the duties and the joys of the full human life." (p. 82)

"THE MORAL RELATION OF PERSON TO PERSON. —If we receive it, that the whole of education consists in the establishment of relations, then, the relations with our fellow-beings must be of the first impor-tance... The solid foundation of *duty* [is] imposed upon us by God, and *due* to each other, whether we will or no. This moral relation of person to person underlies all other relations. We owe it to the past to use its gains worthily and to advance from the point at which it left off. We owe it to the future to prepare a generation better than ourselves. We owe it to the present to *live,* to live with all expansion of heart and soul, all reaching out of our personality towards those relations appointed for us." (p. 84-85)

"THE SENSE OF WHAT IS DUE FROM US DOES NOT COME BY NATURE. —We owe knowledge to the ignorant, comfort to the distressed, healing to the sick, reverence, courtesy and kindness to all men, especially to those with whom we are connected by ties of family or neighborhood; and the sense of these dues does not come by nature." It comes from training and example. (p. 85)

"RELATIONS OF ONESELF WITH ONESELF. —This knowledge is the more important because our power to conduct our relations with other people depends upon our power of conducting our relations with ourselves. Every man carries in his own person the key to human nature, and, in proportion as we are able to use this key, we shall be tolerant, gentle, helpful, wise and reverent..." (p. 86)

"INTIMACY WITH PERSONS OF ALL CLASSES." Children should get to know a variety of people and their different occupations and hobbies. They will then know how to get along with everyone. (p. 87-88)

"RELATION WITH EACH OTHER AS HUMAN BEINGS... Education should have for its aim, not the mastery of certain 'subjects,' but the establishment of these relations in as many directions as circumstances will allow." (p. 88)

"RELATION TO ALMIGHTY GOD." Children should be taught their duty towards God. "It is their duty, that which they *owe,* to love Him 'with all their heart, with all their mind, with all the soul, with all their strength,' these things are seldom taught and understood as they should be." (p. 89)

"We hold that all education is divine, that every good gift of knowledge and insight comes from above, that the Lord the Holy Spirit is the supreme educator of mankind, and that the culmination of all education (which may, at the same time, be reached by a little child) is that personal knowledge of and intimacy with God in which our being finds its fullest perfection." (p. 95)

ALERTNESS —Don't miss chances to serve or be kind. "Seize opportunities of getting knowledge" from the people you meet. "Success in life depends largely upon the cultivation of alertness to seize opportunities, and this is largely a physical habit." (p. 108)

"A CAPTAIN IDEA FOR US, —Education is the Science of Relations. —A child should be brought up to have relations of force with earth and water, should run and ride, swim and skate, lift and carry; should know texture, and work in material; should know by name, and where and how they live at any rate, the things of the earth about him, its birds and beasts and creeping things, its herbs and trees; should be in touch with the literature, art and thought of the past and the present... He must have a living relationship with the present, its historic movement, its science, literature, art, social needs and aspirations. In fact, he must have a wide outlook, intimate relations all round; and force, *virtue,* must pass out of him, whether of hand, will, or sympathy, wherever he touches. This is no impossible program. Indeed it can be pretty well filled in by the time an intelligent boy or girl has reached the age of thirteen or fourteen; for it depends, not upon *how much* is learned, but upon *how* things are learned." (p. 161-162)

"A WIDER CURRICULUM. —Give children a wide range of subjects, with the end in view of establishing in each case some one or more of the relations I have indicated. Let them learn from first-hand sources of information —really good books, the best going, on the subject they are engaged upon. Let them get at the books themselves, and do not let them be flooded with a warm diluent at the lips of their teacher. The teacher's business is to indicate, stimulate, direct and constrain to the acquirement of knowledge, but by no means to be the fountainhead and source of all knowledge. The less parents and teachers talk-in and expound their rations of knowledge and thought to the children they are educating, the better for the children... Children must be allowed to ruminate, must be left alone with their own thoughts. They will ask for help if they want it." (p. 162)

"Let us try, however imperfectly, to make education a science of relationships —in other words, try in one subject or another to let the children work upon living ideas. In this field small efforts are honored with great rewards, and we perceive that the education we are giving exceeds all that we intended or imagined." (p. 162-163)

"OUR AIM IN EDUCATION IS TO GIVE A FULL LIFE. —We owe it to [children] to initiate an immense number of interests... Life should be all *living,* and not merely a tedious passing of time; not all doing or all feeling or all thinking —the strain would be too great —but, all living; that is to say, we should be in touch wherever we go, whatever we hear, whatever we see, with some manner of vital interest. We cannot give the children these interests... The question is not, —how much does the youth *know?* when he has finished his education —but how much does he *care?* and about how many orders of things does he care?... How full is the life he has before him?" (p. 170)

"He gets also when left to himself that real knowledge about each thing he comes across which establishes his relations with that thing. Later, we step in to educate him. In proportion to the range of living relationships we put in his way will he have wide and vital interests and joy in living. His life will be dutiful and serviceable if he is made aware of the laws which rule each relationship; he will learn the laws of work and the joys of work as he perceives that no relation with persons or with things can be kept up without effort.

"Our part is to remove obstructions, to give stimulus and guidance to the child who is trying to get into touch with the universe of things and thoughts. Our error is to suppose that we must act as his showman to the universe, and that there is no community between child and universe except such as we choose to set up." (p. 218-219)

"EDUCATION IS THE SCIENCE OF RELATIONS. —The idea that vivifies teaching...is that *Education is the Science of Relations;* by which phrase we mean that children come into the world with a natural 'appetency,'...for, and affinity with, all the material of knowledge; for interest in the heroic past and in the age of myths; for a desire to know about everything that moves and lives, about strange places and strange peoples; for a wish to handle material and to make; a desire to run and ride and row and do whatever the law of gravitation permits. Therefore we do not feel it is lawful in the early days of a child's life to select certain subjects for his education to the exclusion of others; to say he shall not learn Latin, for example or shall not learn Science; but we endeavor that he shall have relations of pleasure and intimacy established with as many as possible of the interests proper to him; not learning a slight or incomplete smattering about this or that subject, but plunging into vital knowledge, with a great field before him which in all his life he will not be able to explore. In this conception we get that 'touch of emotion' which vivifies knowledge, for it is probable that we *feel* only as we are brought into our proper vital relations." (p. 222-223)

"CHILDREN MUST BE EDUCATED ON BOOKS. —A corollary of the principle that education is the science of relations, is, that no education seems to be worth the name which has not made children at home in the world of books, and so related them, mind to mind, with thinkers who have dealt with knowledge. We reject epitomes, compilations, and their like, and put into children's hands books which, long or short, are *living*. Thus it becomes a large part of the teacher's work to help children to deal with  their books; so that the oral lesson and lecture are but small matters in education, and are used chiefly to summarize or to expand or illustrate... We find...that in working through a considerable book, which may take two or three years to master, the interest of boys and girls is well sustained to the end; they develop an intelligent curiosity as to causes and consequences, and are in fact educating themselves." (p. 226-227)

"...The unspoken demand of children is for a wide and very varied curriculum; it is necessary that they should have some knowledge of the wide range of interests proper to them as human beings, and for no reasons of convenience or time limitations may we curtail their proper curriculum." (Vol. 6, p. 14)

"The children I am speaking of are much occupied with things as well as with books, because 'Education is the Science of Relations,' is the principle which regulates their curriculum; that is, a child goes to school with many aptitudes which he should put into effect. So, he learns a good deal of science, because children have no difficulty in understanding principles, though technical details baffle them. He practices various handicrafts that he may know the feel of wood, clay, leather, and the joy of handling tools, that is, that he may establish a due relation with materials. But, always, it is the book, the knowledge, the clay, the bird or blossom, he thinks of, not his own place or his own progress." (p. 31)

STUDY SUGGESTIONS: Vol. 3, Chapters XVII, XVIII, XIX; Vol. 6, Introduction and Chapter I (if you missed it last month)

Education: The Science of Relations

by Jean Howery

*A*s we read Charlotte Mason's writings, she uses terms with which we are not familiar. So it is with the term "Education is the Science of Relations." I *think* I am starting to understand what she means by this saying as I have read and reread parts of her works. These quotes and views are from Volume 3 of her *Home Education Series.*

Charlotte Mason said, "We may believe that a person—I have a 'baby person' in view—is put into this most delightful world for the express purpose of forming ties of intimacy, joy, association and knowledge with the living and moving things that are therein." (p. 75)

She also stated that to know about something is not the same as knowing something personally. These are her words: "The child who learns his science from a textbook—has no chance of forming relations with things as they are because his kindly obtrusive teacher makes him believe that to know about things is the same thing as knowing them personally." (p. 66)

One of the ways to learn about something is to first get the idea from others. "As an idea comes of the contact of two minds, the idea of another is no more than a *notion* to us until it has undergone a process of generation within us." (p. 70) In other words, until we mull it over in our own mind, the idea does not belong to us. As we claim this idea for *our own,* we act upon it, bringing in the habits we have learned. As we claim it for our own, and we intimately learn all we can about it, the idea becomes a part of our very life.

In very simple terms, let's take the idea of learning about a flower. In the science of relations, we do not just learn to recognize a flower from a textbook, and know it by name. But we learn to recognize it in the field. We smell it. We touch it. And we know where we can find it growing. That in turn leads us to know its seasons, its habits, and to which family it belongs.

Our "knowing" now is a combination of knowledge and of experience with this flower. We know it intimately from both experience and knowledge. It is a part of us and it led us to an even greater search of ideas, knowledge, and experience. It becomes one with us.

I spent a lot of time in the out-of-doors while growing up. Not only did we spend every weekend camping, we annually took a two-week camping vacation. As I was watching a nature movie recently, I came to realize that I had experienced many of the things being shown as part of our wonderful world. I have felt the ocean spray on my face as the tide comes in. I have felt the force of the incoming wave. I have experienced the sand being pulled out from under my feet as the tide goes out.

I've slept out under the stars at night. I've seen shooting stars, not a few, but many. I've seen and recognized by sight and name some of the constellations. I have felt the quiet beauty of the night as I tried to internalize the great expanse of the heavens.

I've slept with a canvas below and on top of me with my brothers and sisters so the morning dew would not get our bedding wet. We remembered to keep our shoes under cover so we didn't have to wake up to damp footwear.

This is the science of relations, to know in my head (to have the knowledge), but also to experience it in my life—with my heart and soul; to speak with feeling and understanding from within as well as from book learning about the wonders of God, or, "subjects" as we call them.

I hope I've been able to do justice to what Miss Mason meant by the term, "Education is the Science of Relations." She truly was a remarkable woman, years ahead of her time. I'm beginning to grasp some of her concepts and philosophy. As I do, I'm grateful to say they continue to expand my views of how I want my children "educated."

The Habit of Attention

Once at a home education convention, we were asked to list ten things after the instructor read a short biography. My mind was blank. I did not have the habit of attention. However, this is a skill easily instilled in children. Here's how to train our children in the habit of attention.

HABIT OF ATTENTION —Our minds go off on tangents. Attention wanders because there are so many things that run through our minds. (Vol. 1, p. 137)

"It is the mother's part to supplement the child's quick observing faculty with the habit of attention. She must see to it that he does not flit from this to that, but looks long enough at one thing to get a real acquaintance with it." This applies to babies and toddlers also. Once the child starts lessons, keep them short and interesting. Don't allow dawdling to even start. You might have to go to a very different subject then come back to the unfinished one after the change. Follow a schedule so child can see that he has only 20 minutes for math, 15 minutes for the next subject, and so forth. If he attends well and gets done early then the time left over is his free time —his reward (natural consequence) for attending. (p. 140)

"VALUE OF NARRATION. —The simplest way of dealing with a paragraph or a chapter is to require the child to narrate its contents after a single attentive reading, —*one* reading, however slow, should be made a condition." (Vol. 3, p. 179)

"Ability —a different thing from genius or talent—is simply the power of fixing the attention steadily on the matter in hand and success in life turns upon this cultivated power far more than on any natural faculty." (Vol. 5, p. 94)

Boredom comes from inattention. Establish the habit of attention. (p. 409)

"Marks, prizes, places, rewards, punishments, praise, blame, or other inducements are not necessary to secure attention, which is voluntary, immediate and surprisingly perfect." (Vol. 6, p. 7)

"We need not labor to get children to learn their lessons; that, if we would believe it, is a matter which nature takes care of. Let the lessons be of the right sort and children will learn them with delight. The call for strenuousness comes with the necessity of forming habits; but here again we are relieved. The intellectual habits of the good life form themselves in the following out of the due curriculum in the right way. As we have already urged, there is but one right way, that is, children must do the work for themselves. They must read the given pages and tell what they have read, they must perform, that is, what we may call *the act of know-ing*. We are all aware, alas, what a monstrous quantity of printed matter has gone into the dustbin of our memories, because we have failed to perform that quite natural and spontaneous 'act of knowing,' as easy to a child as breathing and, if we would believe it, comparatively easy to our-selves. The reward is two-fold: no intellectual habit is so valuable as that of attention; it is a mere habit but it is also the hallmark of an educated person." (p. 99)

"Attention is not the only habit that follows due self-education. The habits of fitting and ready expression, of obedience, of good will, and of an impersonal outlook are spontaneous by-products of education in this sort. So, too, are the habits of right thinking and right judging; while physical habits of neatness and order attend upon the self-respect which follows an education which respects the personality of children." (p. 100)

"Give children the sort of knowledge that they are fitted to assimilate, served in a literary medium, and they will pay great attention." (p. 256)

"I dwell on the single reading because, let me repeat, it is impossible to fix attention on that which we have heard before and know we shall hear again." (p. 261)

STUDY SUGGESTIONS: Vol. 1, Part IV; Vol. 3, Chapter XVI

Narration

$\mathcal{N}$arration is a cornerstone of Charlotte Mason's philosophy of education. It is also a beautiful and easy way to educate children. Soon each of your children will have an impressive collection of narrations.

"CHILDREN MUST LABOR. —This, of getting ideas out of them, is by no means all we must do with books. 'In all labor there is profit,' at any rate in some labor; and the labor of thought is what his book must induce in the child. He must generalize, classify, infer, judge, visualize, discriminate, labor in one way or another, with that capable mind of his, until the substance of his book is assimilated or rejected, according as he shall determine; for the determination rests with him and not with his teacher." (Vol. 3, p. 179)

"VALUE OF NARRATION. —The simplest way of dealing with a paragraph or a chapter is to require the child to narrate its contents after a single attentive reading, —*one* reading, however slow, should be made a condition." (p. 179)

Things that we read only become knowledge as we assimilate it, as our mind acts upon it. We must read with the specific intention to *know* the matter being read. We can read without that effort but it does us no good. (Vol.6, p. 12-13)

Intelligent people *"read to know."* (p. 14) "But, it will be said, reading or hearing various books read, chapter by chapter, and then narrating or writing what has been read or some part of it, —all this is mere memory work. [But one who tries this method on himself]...will find that in the act of narrating every power of his mind comes into play,...that the whole is visualized and brought into relief in an extraordinary way; in fact, that scene or argument has become a part of his personal experience; he *knows*, he has read. *This is not memory work."* (p. 16)

"To secure a conversation or an incident, we 'go over it in our minds;' that is, the mind puts itself through the process of self-questioning... This is what happens in the narrating of a passage read: each new consecutive incident or statement arrives because the mind asks itself, — 'What next?' For this reason it is important that only one reading should be allowed; efforts to memorize weaken the power of attention, the proper activity of the mind; if it is desirable to ask questions in order to emphasize certain points, these should be asked after and not before, or during, the act of narration." (p. 17)

"The intellect requires a moral impulse, and we all stir our minds into action the better if there is an implied 'must' in the background; for children in class the 'must' acts through the *certainty* that they will be required to narrate or write from what they have read with no opportunity of 'looking up,' or other devices of the idle. Children find the act of narrating so pleasurable in itself that urgency on the part of the teacher is seldom necessary." (p. 17)

"The finding of this power which is described as 'sensing a passage,' is as the striking of a vein of gold in that fabulously rich country, human nature. Our 'find' is that children have a natural aptitude for literary expression which they enjoy in hearing or reading and employ in telling or writing." (p. 90)

"As we have already urged, there is but one right way, that is, children must do the work for themselves. They must read the given pages and tell what they have read, they must perform, that is, what we may call the *act of knowing*. We are all aware, alas, what a monstrous quantity of printed matter has gone into the dustbin of our memories, because we have failed to perform that quite natural and spontaneous 'act of knowing,' as easy to a child as breathing and, if we would believe it, comparatively easy to ourselves. The reward is two-fold: no intellectual habit is so valuable as that of attention; it is a mere habit but it is also the hallmark of an educated person." (p. 99)

"A higher education, may be effected more readily by Milton, Gibbon, Shakespeare, Bacon, and a multitude of great thinkers who are therefore great writers... Given absolute attention, and we can do much with four hundred hours a year, but only if we go to work with a certainty that the young students crave knowledge of what we call the 'humanities,' that they read with absolute attention and that, having read, they *know*. They will welcome the preparation for public speaking, an effort for which everyone must qualify in these days, which the act of narration offers." (p. 124)

"Education which demands a *conscious mental effort,* from the scholar, the mental effort of telling again that which has been read or heard. That is how we all learn, we tell again, to ourselves if need be, the matter we wish to retain, the sermon, the lecture, the conversation. The method is as old as the mind of man, the distressful fact is that it has been made so little use of in general education." (p. 159-160)

"Literature at its best is always direct and simple and a normal child of six listens with delight to the tales both of Old and New Testament read to him passage by passage, and by him narrated in turn, with delightful touches of native eloquence." (p. 160)

"The reverent reading of the text, with the following narration, is often curiously word perfect after a single reading; this is the more surprising because we all know how difficult it is to repeat a passage which we have heard a thousand times; the single attentive reading does away with this difficulty and we are able to assure ourselves that children's minds are stored with perfect word pictures of every tender and beautiful scene described in the Gospels." (p. 165)

"We know that young people are enormously interested in the subject [history] and give concentrated attention if we give them the right books. We are aware that our own discursive talk is usually a waste of time and a strain on the scholars' attention, so we confine ourselves to afford-

ing two things, —knowledge, and a keen sympathy in the interest roused by that knowledge. It is our part to see that every child *knows* and *can tell,* whether by way of oral narrative or written essay. In this way an unusual amount of ground is covered with such certainty that no revision is required for the examination at the end of the term. A *single reading* is a condition insisted upon because a naturally desultory habit of mind leads us all to put off the effort of attention as long as a second or third chance of coping with our subject is to be hoped for. It is, however, a mistake to speak of the 'effort of attention.' Complete and entire attention is a natural function which requires no effort and causes no fatigue; the anxious labor of mind of which we are at times aware comes when attention wanders and has again to be brought to the point; but the concentration at which most teachers aim is an innate provision for education and is not the result of training or effort. Our concern is to afford matter of a sufficiently literary character, together with the certainty that no second or third opportunity for knowing a given lesson will be allowed." (p. 171-172)

"The child of six has a definite quantity of consecutive reading, say, forty pages in a term, from a well-written, well-considered, large volume which is also well-illustrated. Children cannot of course themselves read a book which is by no means written down to the 'child's level' so the teacher reads and the children 'tell' paragraph by paragraph, passage by passage. The teacher does not talk much and is careful never to interrupt a child who is called upon to 'tell.' The first efforts may be stumbling but presently the children get into their 'stride' and 'tell' a passage at length with surprising fluency. The teacher probably allows other children to correct any faults in the telling when it is over. The teacher's own really difficult part is to keep up sympathetic interest by look and occasional word, by remarks upon a passage that has been narrated, by occasional showing pictures, and so on. But she will bear in mind that the child of six has begun the serious business of his education, that it does not matter much whether he understands this word or that, but that it matters a great deal that he should learn to deal directly with books.

Whatever a child or grown-up person can tell, that we may be sure he knows, and what he cannot tell, he does not know.... Now a passage to be memorized requires much conning, much repetition, and meanwhile the learners are 'thinking' about other matters, that is, the *mind* is not at work in the act of memorizing. To read a passage with full attention and to tell it afterwards has a curiously different effect... [There is] the happy distinction between *word* memory and *mind* memory, which, once the force of it is realized, should bring about sweeping changes in our methods of education.

"Trusting to mind memory we visualize the scene, are convinced by arguments, take pleasure in the turn of the sentences and frame our own upon them; in fact that particular passage or chapter has been received into us and become a part of us just as literally as was yesterday's dinner; nay, more so, for yesterday's dinner is of little account tomorrow; but several months, perhaps years hence, we shall be able to narrate the passage we had, so to say, consumed and grown upon with all the vividness, detail and accuracy of the first telling. All those powers of the mind...have been brought into play in dealing with the intellectual matter thus afforded; so we may not ask questions to help the child to reason, paint fancy pictures to help him to imagine, draw out moral lessons to quicken his conscience. These things take place as involuntarily as processes of digestion." (p. 172)

"While we grown-up persons read and forget because we do not take the pains to *know* as we read, these young students have the powers of perfect recollection and just application because they have read with attention and concentration and have in every case reproduced what they have read in narration, or, the gist of some portion of it, in writing." (p. 185)

"Teachers err out of their exceeding good-will and generous zeal. They feel that they cannot do too much for children and attempt to do for them those things which they are richly endowed to do for themselves. Among these is the art of composition, that art of 'telling' which culminates in a Scott or a Homer... The grown-up who writes the tale to their 'telling' will cover many pages before getting to the end of 'Hans and Gretel' or 'The Little Match Girl' or a Bible story. The facts are sure to be accurate and the expression surprisingly vigorous, striking and unhesitating. Probably few grown-ups could 'tell' one of Aesop's *Fables* with the terse directness which children reproduce. Neither are the children's narrations incoherent; they go on with their book, week by week, whatever comes at a given time,...from the point where they left off, —and there never is a time when their knowledge is scrappy.

"...For all their work lends itself to oral composition and the power of such composition is innate in children and is not the result of instruction... Young children should be allowed to narrate paragraph by paragraph, which children of seven or eight will 'tell' chapter by chapter. Corrections must not be made during the act of narration, nor must any interruption be allowed." (p. 190-191)

"From their earliest days they should get the habit of reading literature which they should take hold of for themselves, much or little, in their own way. As the object of every writer is to explain himself in his own book, the child and the author must be trusted together, without the intervention of the middleman. What his author does not tell him he must go without knowing for the present. No explanation will really help him, and explanations of words and phrases spoil the text and should not be attempted unless children ask, What does so and so mean? when other children in the class will probably tell." (p. 191-192)

"Composition is not an adjunct but an integral part of their education in every subject... But let me again say there must be no attempt to teach composition. Our failure as teachers is that we place too little dependence on the intellectual power of our scholars, and as they are modest little souls what the teacher kindly volunteers to do for them, they feel that they cannot do for themselves. But give them a fair field and no favor and they will describe their favorite scene from the play they have read, and much besides." (p. 192)

"Having been brought up so far upon stylists the [older] pupils are almost certain to have formed a good style; because they have been thrown into the society of *many* great minds, they will not make a servile copy of any one but will shape an individual style out of the wealth of material they possess; and because they have matter in abundance and of the best they will not write mere verbiage." (p. 194)

"Give children the sort of knowledge that they are fitted to assimilate, served in a literary medium, and they will pay great attention. What next? A clever *questionnaire*? Questions...are an intrusion and a bore; but here we have a word of ancient wisdom for our guidance. 'The mind can know nothing except what it can express in the form of an answer to a question put by the mind to itself.' Observe, not a question put by an outsider, but, put by the mind to itself. We all know the trick of it. If we want to tell the substance of a conversation, a sermon, a lecture, we 'go over it in our minds' first and the mind puts its question to itself... What next? —and lo, we have it, the whole thing complete!" (p. 256-258)

"Given a book of literary quality suitable to their age and children will know how to deal with it without elucidation. Of course they will not be able to answer questions because questions are an impertinence which we all resent, but they will tell you the whole thing with little touches of individual personality in the narrative. Let the boy read and he knows, that is, if he must tell again what he has read.

"This, of telling again, sounds very simple but it is really a magical creative process by means of which the narrator sees what he has conceived, so definite and so impressive is the act of narrating that which has been read only once. I dwell on the single reading because, let me repeat, it is impossible to fix attention on that which we have heard before and know we shall hear again.

"Treat children in this reasonable way, mind to mind; not so much the mind of the teacher to that of the child, —that would be to exercise undue influence —but the minds of a score of thinkers who meet the children mind to mind, in their several books, the teacher performing the graceful office of presenting the one enthusiastic mind to the other. In this way children cover an incredible amount of ground in the time at their disposal." (p. 260-261)

"The knowledge of God is the principal knowledge, and no teaching of the Bible which does not further that knowledge is of religious value. Therefore the children read, or if they are too young to read for themselves the [parent] reads to them, a passage of varying length covering an incident or some definite teaching... The children narrate what has been read after the reading; they do this with curious accuracy and yet with some originality, conveying the spiritual teaching which the teacher has indicated. Now this is no parrot-exercise, but is the result of such an assimilation of the passage that it has become a part of the young scholar." (p. 272-273)

STUDY SUGGESTIONS: Vol. 3, Chapter XVI; Vol. 6, Introduction, Chapter X (p. 190-208)

The Power of Narration

Something very exciting occurred in our home school during the fall of 1994. We discovered the power of narration. I believe in delaying academics until children are ready which is usually a bit later than most people realize. But surely by age ten, my avid reader would also be a writer? April wrote a few letters to friends and more rarely short entries in her journal. But when asked to write a story or an essay, her attempts were not even close to grade level.

I've known about narration for years. But I've also known my children for years. I could picture their response to mom's latest request. Finally, I decided that no matter how rebelliously it was received by the children, we were going to attempt narration as put forth by Charlotte Mason.

One of the main practices of Miss Mason's philosophy of education is narrating from whole, "living" books. Think about the skill that it takes to fill in blanks or choose from a list of multiple choices. Now imagine having to retell a story you've just heard or read. Which requires a higher level of thinking? That which we put into our own words, becomes our own. It is retained.

April and I took turns reading *Squanto, Friend of the Pilgrims* by Clyde Robert Bulla. After reading the first chapter, I narrated, or told back, in a couple of sentences the gist of the chapter. Complaints rained on me when I said that April and her younger brother would retell subsequent chapters. So I gave them the choice of oral narration or written. April opted to write. And write she did! Amazingly, three handwritten pages appeared after we read almost half the book. She remembered many details. The story became hers.

The power of narration gave a child her first real success with writing. April was self-motivated and enthusiastic. I never dreamed that she would actually enjoy this. Or that she would write so much. Or that the quality of her writ-

ing would improve so dramatically with the first attempt. Then it dawned on me that in the past, she just didn't know what to say. Perhaps as a beginning writer, it's easier to write when drawing from the work of an accomplished author. April finished reading Squanto on her own. Her completed story was eleven handwritten pages. I typed it for her, correcting spelling and punctuation as I went.

Colton refused to cooperate, so we compromised. He chose a different book for me to read to him. Perhaps *The Dragonslayers* by Bruce Coville doesn't qualify as a "living book" in the best literary sense, but we enjoyed it. After reading each chapter, Colton reluctantly summed them up in a sentence or two that he dictated to me. Dad was impressed when he read the beginning of Colton's story a couple nights later. That parental praise may have spurred him on because the next day, Colton was talking so fast that I couldn't keep up. Instead of a begrudging sentence, he was retelling the chapter in an animated paragraph. He now has a sense of accomplishment and proud ownership with a copy of his narration in his possession. He even gave copies of it away at his birthday party, inspiring his friends to start telling narrations to their mothers.

My kindergarten-age son, Logan, caught the spirit. He narrated Kipling's "The Elephant Child." We didn't have a picture book version. But he stayed attentive and produced a lovely story. Notice in his story how the image of the crocodile winking his eyes struck Logan's fancy. In Kipling's story, the young elephant returns to his family and spanks them all with his newly formed trunk. Logan's story ends with his vision of a loving reunion of the elephant child with his family. This is just one example of how children make the retelling their own and not a parrot-imitation.

Another time with this same child, we tried narrating "Puss in Boot." But that didn't work. The story followed two different characters. This proved to be too complicated for him. For younger children, read stories that are linear as they follow only one character's point of view.

Charlotte Mason suggested having children narrate, or describe: a painting; a wild flower and where it was found; the life story of a butterfly after keeping a caterpillar; a view in the countryside or seashore from memory (not while looking at it). Stories directly from the Bible, poems, biographies, histories, as well as good fiction, can be sources of narration.

Adapt the basic concept of narration to meet your children's needs. This method works as well for the seventeen-year-old as it does for the six. Be flexible and innovative. Ask a thought-provoking question to stimulate discussion. Have children list a half dozen facts they learned from a reading. Or they could illustrate a descriptive passage. Writing with a goal in mind may provide motivation; bind narrations into books as keepsakes or gifts. But be brave and give narration a try. You may also witness the miraculous power of narration in the education of your children.

The Elephant's Child

by Logan Gardner, age 6

The elephant wanted to know what crocodiles eat for supper. So the elephant went to the river to see what they eat.

The crocodile winked with one eye and then with the other eye. The elephant said, "I just want to know what crocodiles eat."

The crocodile said, "Come here and I'll tell you."

The elephant got close. Then the crocodile bit his nose. The crocodile pulled. And the elephant pulled the other way. The elephant's nose got longer and longer when they both pulled.

The elephant got away. Then the elephant went home to his mother and father and brothers and sisters. He kissed them all.

The Beauty of Narration

by Jean Howery

One of my neighbors commented on how well Shawn, my seven-year-old, speaks. Her son is the same age and is a good reader. Shawn, however, is a non-reader. He's working at phonics but really is a non-reader. What we do, though, is a lot of narration. Narration, simply put, is the telling back of what has been read to you or what you have just read.

Even before I knew "narration" is what we were doing, my children have either been telling me or repeating back to me what I was reading to them. I did it at first to see if they understood what was happening in the story. Not that I was testing them; it was never meant as a critique. I just wanted to make sure they were following the story line—if they understood what was going on.

Now I find out that is a very good thing to have your children do. When they can repeat back what it is they have heard or read, it's as if it puts the story in the first person. They internalize what the message is, what it is the main character is learning deep inside.

Of course, this presumes you are reading books that have substance to them. Stories that teach values, such as integrity, honesty, hard work, saying you're sorry, being able to take an honest look at yourself. Charlotte Mason called these "living books." (Stories such as "Jane and Dick ran after the ball," just don't cut it as far as offering ideals to emulate, if those can even be called "stories." Perhaps "readers" is a better term for reading material such as that.)

Even as two-year-olds, we were having our children repeat back to us what we just read to them. Usually this is at scripture study time. It really has helped to build their vocabulary and speaking skills. I think it

has also helped them be comfortable with speaking aloud in front of people.

According to Charlotte Mason, age six is soon enough to actually have your child narrate back to you. In *The Home Education Series,* Vol. 1,

Charlotte says, "Until he is six, let Bobbie narrate only when and what he has a mind to. ...Narrating is an art, like poetry-making or painting, because it is there in every child's mind, waiting to be discovered, and is not the result of any process of disciplinary education."

If we think about that, it is so true. If we will only "let" them, a child will talk our leg off. This really is a gift which our children are endowed with, the art of being able to explain what it is they have seen or heard or just learned. We need to take seriously the talk of our young children and listen as often as we can to the "tellings," even if we cannot fully understand it. They fully understand what it is they are relating to us. The respect we give to them as we listen, not only with our ears but with our minds and hearts as well, will surely instill a confidence in them that what they have to say is important. Then as they get older and narrate to us, the story they have just retold to us also has meaning and importance to themselves as well.

We have an old book set that has quite a few biographies in it. I chose *Joan of Arc* to read to the children for narration. Shawn retold to me the story. I was amazed at his retention level! He not only kept the story line in order, he remembered what was said so well, one would think he was quoting from the book. I wrote down as he narrated and we ended with almost three handwritten pages. He decided to draw a picture to illustrate his story. Only in one instance, did I help him. That was in remembering the uncrowned king's name. Here is a sampling from that narration:

A year passed. Joan heard the voices again, "Be a good girl. God will show you how to save France."

She cut her hair off and dressed like a boy. She had pants on and a cap and a shirt. She went to the gates of the castle. She told them her message. They asked the captain to let her in and the captain did. There were two guards beside her. Soon they got to the big rock which on top was the castle.

She went in. She saw some women but they did not help her find the uncrowned King Charles. She found him and knelt down to him, and told him her message-the voices she heard and that they came from God.

I must admit, I have a hard time not running for a pencil every time Shawn starts to tell me something. I do want to keep a record of his narration, though. It's a tangible product that shows "his own school work," in spite of the fact that he is not yet reading.

In fact, Grandma and Grandpa were here visiting from St. George just a few days ago. Shawn brought out his *Joan of Arc* book and showed it to Grandpa. Grandpa is not very pleased that Shawn is not reading yet. I really do try not to let other people's opinions determine my own views of my child's progress, but I also don't want them to think my children are not "smart or are not learning" just because they are not doing such and such by a certain age.

I was very happy for Shawn when Grandpa was impressed on how well Shawn was able to narrate back what he had heard in the story. Joan of Arc was not afraid to take action, no matter what others said or thought. I am happy that Shawn has heard and knows "firsthand in his own mind" of another person who stood up for what she believe in. To me, that is the beauty of narration.

Narration in Summer Education

*A*re you looking for something a little different to do this summer? You don't want your kids to get out of the habit of learning at home but you want something laid back and easy to do. Summer is the perfect time to start implementing narration in your home school.

Imagine your child lounging on the lawn chair as he retells a story you read to him. Or your older child comes to you after finishing a book she was really into; now she wants to tell you all about it. Or your five-year-old describes the setting of the family vacation you just enjoyed together.

Narration is an important part of a method of education started by Charlotte Mason around the turn of the century. I've known about the Mason Method for years but had never incorporated it beyond reading aloud. I thought my children would refuse to cooperate. But this simple and beautiful concept of narration has literally been a miracle in our home school.

We have a relaxed structure in our home school. I have had many experiences that have supported my belief in delaying academics. However, I was beginning to be concerned about my fifth grade daughter, April. She was virtually a non-writer (although an avid reader) except for notes to me expressing her feelings or a couple of short letters to friends. Not wanting to instill an aversion to writing, I didn't push. Then we discovered the wonderful qualities of narration.

The miracle of narration gave a child her first real success with writing. After reading *Squanto, Friend of the Pilgrims* by Clyde Robert Bulla, April wrote eleven pages full of details. She was self-motivated and enthusiastic. The quality of her writing improved dramatically with this first attempt at narration. As a beginning writer, it's easier to write when drawing from the work of an accomplished author who has already done the work of figuring out what to write. A well-crafted book is turned into an original retelling.

Students in Charlotte Mason schools read thousands of pages a year. They were able to summarize any of it as a final exam.

Cramming was impossible; students retained the information with just one reading. That which we put into our own words, becomes our own. It is retained.

I read another of Bulla's books to my children. When we were through with *Eagle Feather*, I asked Colton, age eight, to narrate the story to me. He was reluctant at first, saying he couldn't remember the story. I helped draw the first sentence out of him. Then I spent the next three pages saying, "Slow down. I can't type that fast."

Each person gets something different from a reading. Some ideas or images catch in the mind. Retelling brings the perspective of the individual into the story. Although the narration is inspired by the written work of another, the end product is an original piece.

Charlotte Mason emphasized using "living" books as sources for narration. This means we read the best written, most uplifting, inspiring works we can find. Many classics fit this description. So do Shakespeare and the Bible. Narration sources can be fiction, biographies and other non-fiction, poetry, or plays.

If you have younger children or have never done narration before, I recommend starting with one of these books: *The Aesop for Children, Sword in the Tree, The Courage of Sarah Noble, The Cabin Faced West, The Light at Tern Rock, The Hundred Dresses, The Glorious Flight, The Matchlock Gun, Benjamin West and his Cat Grimalkin,* or *Christian Liberty's Nature Readers*. For older children or families accustomed to reading aloud try: *The Trumpeter of Krakow; Johnny Tremain; The Golden Goblet; Kidnapped; The Hobbit; The Chronicles of Narnia; Carry On, Mr. Bowditch;* or *The Door in the Wall.*

Adapt the basic concept of narration to meet your children's needs. This method works for all ages of children. If you squat down to listen to

a three-year-old's excited chatter about what his puppy just did, that's narration. If someone summarizes yesterday's listening before starting the next chapter of the book the family is reading aloud, that's narration. If a child draws a picture depicting the Bible story just heard, that's narration. If a group does an impromptu rendition of a Shakespearean play, that's narration.

By the fall, your children will be experienced narrators. Their speaking skills may have improved; their tellings will be more coherent.

Older students may be ready to make the transition to written narrations, although oral narrations should continue on a regular basis. Like me, you may choose to fix spelling and punctuation errors yourself as you type the stories. By keeping spelling and grammar lessons separate from narration, children will be able to focus on getting their thoughts down on paper. They will improve naturally the more they write.

But right now it's summer. Have a vacation. Back off from academic concerns. Enjoy some good books together. So go relax in a lawn chair and work on your tan while your child gives you an oral narration. After all, it is summertime.

The Way of the Will

Our will power is a potentially powerful tool we each have at our disposal. We must exercise it like a muscle and teach our children to do the same.

The Will —The Conscience —The Divine Life in the Child (this section has lots of good material, especially the part about the Will) The Will —When we say a child is willful, he really lacks the power of will to control himself. (Vol. 1, Part VI)

"And here is the line which divides the effective from the non-effective people, the great from the small, the good from the well-intentioned and respectable; it is in proportion as a man has self-controlling, self-compelling power that he is able to do, even of his own pleasure; that he can depend upon himself, and be sure of his own action in emergencies." (p. 323)

WAY OF THE WILL —Learn to control your will by use of *incentives.* ex: If I buckle down and get this done, then I can do something fun. Think of something else *diversion and control of thoughts. Good habits* are allies of the will. Every effort of *obedience* should give child a sense of conquest over his own inclinations and strengthen his habits of self-management and self-restraint. (p. 234)

"'I am' —we have the power of knowing ourselves. 'I ought' —we have within us a moral judge [our conscience], to whom we feel ourselves subject, and who points out and requires of us our duty. 'I can' — we are conscious of power to do that which we perceive we ought to do. 'I will' —we determine to exercise that power with a volition which is in itself a step in the execution of that which we will." (p. 330)

"The great things of life, life itself, are not easy of definition. The Will, we are told, is 'the sole practical faculty of man.' But who is to define the Will? We are told again that 'the Will is the man;' and yet most men go through life without a single definite act of willing. Habit, convention, the customs of the world have done so much for us that we get up, dress, breakfast, follow our morning's occupations, our later relaxations, without an act of choice. For this much at any rate we know about the will. Its function is to *choose,* to decide, and there seems to be no doubt that the greater becomes the effort of decision,  the weaker grows the general will... But the one achievement possible and necessary for every man is character, and character is as finely wrought metal beaten into shape and beauty by the repeated and accustomed action of will. We who teach should make it clear to ourselves that our aim in education is less conduct than character; conduct may be arrived at, as we have seen, by indirect routes, but it is of value to the world only as it has its source in character." (Vol. 6, p. 128-129)

"What we do *with the will* we describe as voluntary. What we do *without the* conscious action of *will* is involuntary. The will has only one mode of action, its function is to 'choose,' and with every choice we make we grow in force of character." (p. 129)

"His will is the safeguard of a man against the unlawful intrusion of other persons. We are taught that there are offenses against the bodies of others which may not be committed, but who teaches us that we may not intrude upon the minds and overrule the wills of others; that it is indecent to let another probe the thoughts of the 'unconscious mind' whether of child or man? Now the thought that we choose is commonly the thought that we ought to think and the part of the teacher is to afford to each child a full reservoir of the right thought of the world to draw from. For right thinking is by no means a matter of *self*-expression. Right thought flows upon the stimulus of an idea, and ideas are stored as we have seen in books and pictures and the lives of men and nations; these instruct the conscience and stimulate the will, and man or child *chooses.*" (p. 130)

"[The child] recognizes that a strong will is not synonymous with 'being good,' nor with a determination to have your own way. He learns to distribute the characters he comes across in his reading on either side of a line, those who are willful and those who are governed by will; and this line by no means separates between the bad and the good.

"It does divide, however, between the impulsive, self-pleasing, self-seeking, and the persons who have an aim beyond and outside of themselves... It follows for him that he must not only *will*, but will with a view to an object outside himself... The will, too, is of slow growth, nourished upon the ideas proposed to it, and so all things work together for good to the child who is duly educated... The simple rectified will, what our Lord calls 'the single eye,' would appear to be the one thing needful for straight living and serviceableness. But always the first condition of will, good or ill, is an object outside of self... A king is not a king unless he reigns and a man is less than a man unless he wills. Another thing to be observed is that even the constant will has its times of rise and fall, and one of the secrets of living is how to tide over the times of fall in will power." (p. 131-132)

"Once again, the will is the man. The business of the will is to choose. There are many ways to get out of the task of choosing but it is always, — 'Choose you this day whom ye will serve.' There are two services open to us all, the service of God, (including that of man) and the service of self. If our aim is just to get on, 'to do ourselves well,' to get all possible ease, luxury and pleasure out of our lives, we are serving self and for the service of self, no act of will is required. Our appetites and desires are always at hand to spur us into the necessary exertions. But if we serve God and our neighbor, we have to be always on the watch to choose between the ideas that present themselves." (p. 134)

"Shall we take an idea in or reject it? Conscience and reason have their say, but *will* is supreme and the behavior of will is determined by all the principles we have gathered, all the opinions we have formed. We accept the notion, ponder it. At first we vaguely intend to act upon it; then we form a definite purpose, then a resolution and then comes an act or general temper of mind." (p. 134)

"A change of physical or mental occupation is very good for the overstrained will, but if no other change is convenient, let us *think* of something else, no matter how trifling... The will does not want the support of arguments but the recreation of rest, change, diversion. In a surprisingly short time it is able to return to the charge and to choose this day the path of duty, however dull or tiresome, difficult or dangerous. The 'way of the will' is a secret of power, the secret of self-government, with which people should be furnished, not only for ease in practical right doing, or for advance in the religious life, but also for their intellectual well-being. Our claim to free will is a righteous claim; will can only be free, whether its object be right or wrong; it is a matter of choice and there is no choice but free choice. But we are apt to translate free will into free thought... Our thoughts are not our own and we are not free to think as we choose. The injunction, — 'Choose ye this day,' applies to the thoughts which we allow ourselves to receive." (p. 136-137)

"The ordering of the will is not an affair of sudden resolve; it is the outcome of a slow and ordered education in which precept and example flow in from the lives and thoughts of other men, men of antiquity and men of the hour, as unconsciously and spontaneously as the air we breathe. But the moment of choice is immediate and the act of the will voluntary; and the object of education is to prepare us for this immediate choice and voluntary action which every day presents.

"While affording some secrets of 'the way of the will' to young people, we should perhaps beware of presenting the ideas of 'self-knowledge, self-reverence, and self-control.' All adequate education must be outward bound, and the mind which is concentrated upon self-emolument, even though it be the emolument of all the virtues, misses the higher and the simpler secrets of life. Duty and service are the sufficient motives for the arduous training of the will that a child goes through with little consciousness. The gradual fortifying of the will which many a schoolboy undergoes is hardly perceptible to himself however tremendous the results may be for his city or his nation. Will, free will, must have an object outside of self; and the poet has said the last word so far as we yet know, —

'Our wills are ours we know not how; Our wills are our to make them Thine.'" (p. 137)

STUDY SUGGESTIONS: Vol. 1, Part VI, Chapters I and II; Vol. 4, Part II; Vol. 6, Chapter VIII.

The Way of Reason

We need to be cautious of our sense of reasoning as it may lead to rationalization. We strive to develop right reasoning ourselves and to help our children do the same.

"We cannot give a better training in right reasoning than by letting children work out the arguments in favor of this or that conclusion." (Vol. 6, p. 140)

"It is worth while to ask a child, How did you think of it? when he comes to tell you of a new game he has invented, a new country of the imagination he has named, peopled and governed. He will probably tell you what first 'put it into his head' and then how the reasons one after another came to him. After, —How did *you* think of it? —the next question that will occur to a child is, —How did *he* think of it? —and he will distinguish between the first notion that has 'put it into his head' and the reasoned steps which have gone to the completion of an object, the discovery of a planet, the making of a law... Children should know that such things are before them also; that whenever they want to do wrong capital reasons for doing the wrong thing will occur to them. But, happily, when they want to do right no less cogent reasons for right doing will appear." (p. 141-142)

"After abundant practice in reasoning and tracing out the reasons of others, whether in fact or fiction, children may readily be brought to the conclusions that reasonable and right are not synonymous terms; that reason is their servant, not their ruler... Reason is not to be trusted with the government of a man, much less that of a state; because well-reasoned arguments are brought into play for a wrong course as for a right. He will see that reason works involuntarily; that all the beautiful steps follow one another in his mind without any activity or intention on his own part; but he need never suppose that he was hurried along into evil by thoughts which he could not help, because reason never begins it. It is only when he chooses to think about some course or plan...that reason comes into play; so, if he chooses to think about a purpose that is good, many excellent reasons will hurry up to support him; but, alas, if he choose to entertain a wrong notion, he, as it were, rings the bell for reason, which enforces his wrong intention with a score of arguments proving that wrong is right." (p. 142)

"For logic gives us the very formula of reason, and that which is logically proved is not necessarily right... [Children should grow] up cognizant of the beauty and wonder of the act of reasoning, and also, of the limitations which attend it." (p. 144)

"But the function of education is not to give technical skill but to develop a person; the more of a person, the better the work of whatever kind... But they must follow arguments and detect fallacies for themselves. Reason like the other powers of the mind, requires material to work upon whether embalmed in history and literature, or afloat with the news of a strike or uprising. It is madness to let children face a debatable world with only, say, a mathematical preparation. If our business were to train their power of reasoning, such a training would no doubt be of service; but the power is there already, and only wants material to work upon.

"This caution must be borne in mind. Reason, like all other properties of a person, is subject to habit and works upon the material it is accustomed to handle." (p. 147)

"What are we to do? Are we to waste time in discussing with children every idle and blasphemous proposition that comes their way? Surely not. But we may help them to principles which should enable them to discern these two characters for themselves." (p. 148)

"Children must know that we cannot prove any of the great things of life, not even that we ourselves live; but we must rely upon that which we know without demonstration... Once we are convinced of the fallibility of our own reason we are able to detect the fallacies in the reasoning of our opponents and are not liable to be carried away by every wind of doctrine." (p. 150)

STUDY SUGGESTIONS: Vol. 4, Part II, Chapter VI (p. 56); Vol. 6, Chapter IX (p. 139)

Goals of Education

What should be our goals in education? Charlotte Mason discussed these at length. Here are some goals we could strive for.

"THE GREAT HUMAN RELATIONSHIPS. —Perhaps the main part of a child's education should be concerned with the great human relationships..." (Vol. 3, p. 80)

"THE MORAL RELATION OF PERSON TO PERSON. —If we receive it, that the whole of education consists in the establishment of relations, then, the relations with our fellow-beings must be of the first importance..." (p. 84)

"We hold that all education is divine, that every good gift of knowledge and insight comes from above, that the Lord the Holy Spirit is the supreme educator of mankind, and that the culmination of all education (which may, at the same time, be reached by a little child) is that personal knowledge of and intimacy with God in which our being finds its fullest perfection." (p. 95)

"HIGH IDEALS. —It is time we set ourselves seriously to this work of moral education which is to be done, most of all, by presenting the children with high ideals. 'Lives of great men all remind us we can make our lives sublime,' and the study of the lives of great men and of the great moments in the lives of smaller men is most wonderfully inspiring to children, especially when they perceive the strenuousness of the childhood out of which a noble manhood has evolved itself. As one grows older no truth strikes one more than that 'the child is father to the man.'" (p. 133)

"We do not sufficiently realize the

need for unity of principle in education. Our positive purpose is to present, in season and out of season, one such universal idea; that is, that education is the science of relations." (p. 160-161)

"It is as true for children as for ourselves that, the wider the range of interests, the more intelligent is the apprehension of each." (p. 209)

"Education should aim at giving knowledge 'touched with emotion.'" (p. 220)

"KNOWLEDGE VERSUS INFORMATION... Great minds...are able to deal at first hand with appearances or experiences; the ordinary mind gets a little of its knowledge by such direct dealing, but for the most part it is set in action by the vivifying knowledge of others, which is at the same time a stimulus and a point of departure. The information acquired in the course of education is only by chance, and here and there, of practical value. Knowledge, on the other hand, that is, the product of the vital action of the mind on the material presented to it, is power; as it implies an increase of intellectual aptitude in new directions, and an always new point of departure.

"Perhaps the chief function of a teacher is to distinguish information from knowledge in the acquisitions of his pupils. Because knowledge is power, the child who has got knowledge will certainly show power in dealing with it. He will recast, condense, illustrate, or narrate with vividness and with freedom in the arrangement of his words." (p. 224)

"Our aim in education is to give children vital interests in as many directions as possible...because the crying evil of the day is, it seems to me, intellectual inanition." (p. 231)

"RELATIONS AND INTERESTS. —I have throughout spoken of '*Relations*,' and not of '*Interests*,' because interests may be casual, unworthy, and passing. Everyone, even the most ignorant, has interests of a sort; while to make valid any one relation, implies that knowledge has begun in, at any rate, that one direction. But the defect in our educational thought is that we have ceased to realize that knowledge is vital; and, as children and adults, we suffer from underfed minds." (p. 241)

"The getting of knowledge and the getting of delight in knowledge are the ends of a child's education." (p. 242)

"Education by Books. —For the last twelve years we have tried the plan of bringing children up on *Books* and *Things,* and, on the whole, the results are pleasing. The average child studies with 'delight.' We do not say he will remember all he knows, but, to use a phrase of Jane Austen's, he will have had his 'imagination warmed' in many regions of knowledge." (p. 243)

"It is the old story; utilitarian education [only what is useful to help us earn a living] is profoundly immoral, in that it defrauds a child of the associations which should give him intellectual atmosphere." (Vol. 5, p. 313)

"Casual reading—that is, vague reading round a subject without the effort *to know*—is not our goal... If we are to read and grow thereby, we must read to *know,* that is, our reading must be study—orderly, definite, purposeful." (p. 382)

"A person is not built up from without but from within, that is, he is *living,* and all external educational appliances and activities which are intended to mold his character are decorative and not vital." (p. 23)

"No one knoweth the things of a man but the spirit of a man which is in him; therefore, there is no education but self-education, and as soon as a young child begins his education he does so as a student. Our business is to give him mind-stuff, and both quality and quantity are essential. Naturally, each of us possesses this mind-stuff only in limited measure, but we know where to procure it; for the best thought the world possesses is stored in books; we must open books to children, the best books; our own concern is abundant provision and orderly serving." (p. 26)

"People are naturally divided into those who read and think and those who do not read or think; and the business of schools is to see that all their scholars shall belong to the former class; it is worth while to remember that thinking is inseparable from reading which is concerned with the content of a passage and not merely with the printed matter." (p. 31)

"In urging a method of self-education for children...I should like to dwell on the enormous relief to teachers; ...the difference is just that between driving a horse that is light and a horse that is heavy in hand; the former covers the ground of his own gay will and the driver goes merrily. The teacher who allows his scholars the freedom of the city of books is at liberty to be their guide, philosopher and friend; and is no longer the mere instrument of forcible intellectual feeding." (p. 32)

"Education, like faith, is the evidence of things not seen... The only fit sustenance for the mind is ideas... Our business is to give children the great ideas of life, of religion, history, science; but it is the *ideas* we must give, clothed upon with facts as they occur, and must leave the child to deal with these as he chooses." (p. 39-40)

"Few of the offices of education are more important than that of preparing men to distinguish between their rights and their duties. We each have our rights and other persons have their duties towards us as we towards them; but it is not easy to learn that we have precisely the same rights as other people and no more; that other people owe to us just such duties as we owe to them... But our eyes must be taught to see, and hence the need for all the processes of education, futile in proportion as they do not serve this end. To think fairly requires, we know, knowledge as well as consideration." (p. 60)

"[The] contention is, given a well-educated man with cultivated imagination, trained judgment, wide interests, and he is prepared to master the intricacies of any profession; while he knows at the same time how to make use of himself, of the powers with which nature and education have endowed him for his own happiness; the delightful employment of his leisure; for the increased happiness of his neighbors and the well-being of the community; that is, such a man is able, not only to earn his living, but to *live.* " (p. 121)

"This is the way to make great men and not by petty efforts to form character in this direction or in that. Let us take it to ourselves that great character comes out of great thoughts, and that great thought must be initiated by great thinkers; then we shall have a definite aim in education." (p. 278)

"If knowledge means so much to us, 'What is knowledge?' the reader asks. We can give only a negative answer. Knowledge is not instruction, information, scholarship, a well-stored memory. It is passed, like the light of a torch, from mind to mind, and the flame can be kindled at original minds only. Thought, we know, breeds thought; it is as a vital thought touches our minds that our ideas are vitalized, and out of our ideas comes our conduct of life." (p. 303)

STUDY SUGGESTIONS: Vol. 3, Chapters XIV, XV, XX, XXI, XXII; Vol. 6, Chapter VI (p. 94) or if ambitious all of Vol. 6.

Third Time's a Charm

Book Review of For the Children's Sake

I recently read *For the Children's Sake* by Susan Schaeffer Macauley for the third time. I had read it twice before over the years. However, this last time I read the book it had much more meaning for me because I had finally been incorporating aspects of Charlotte Mason's teachings into our home school. It was the right time in my development for its message to sink deeply in my mind.

Susan starts out discussing her search for a proper education for her daughters. She was living in England at the time and came across a Charlotte Mason school run out of a cottage. It was the answer to her prayers.

Mrs. Macauley says, "Look well at the child on your knee. In whatever condition you find him, look with reverence. We can only love and serve him and be his friend. We cannot own him. He is not ours." (p. 132)

"Education: A Science of Relationships" is the sixth chapter and probably my favorite. It touches on various subjects and how they relate to the child. There are lots of practical suggestions.

For the Children's Sake is a good introduction to Charlotte Mason's philosophy of education. It is easy to read and fairly short—about 160 pages. It goes through each of the 18 points Miss Mason made in her "Short Synopsis."

A friend of mine borrowed my copy of *For the Children's Sake* for a few days. She decided to hurry and read it again before returning it because she thought it so wonderful. I guess for some of us a second reading is needed but for me the third time was the charm.

❧

A Charlotte Mason Companion

Review of a book by Karen Andreola

Karen Andreola, a giant name in Charlotte Mason circles, has written a lovely book—*A Charlotte Mason Companion: Personal Reflections on the Gentle Art of Learning*. The format is visually appealing with generous illustrations. The content is substantial and well written. Karen shares her personal experiences based on years of research and application. She makes us feel like we, too, will have success using Miss Mason's approach.

Karen's chapters on parenting, using whole books, and encouraging narrations give us some great advice. She covers many topics: composition, vocabulary, spelling, grammar, the arts, poetry, history, nature study, and even some handiwork ideas. This book is user-friendly with lots of practical information presented in a warm and honest manner.

Karen writes, "Believe in God, believe in your children, believe in Charlotte's principle for a gentle art of learning, and you will find joy."

This book may become our frequent and favorite companion as we open our minds and hearts to a wonderful philosophy of education. Karen Andreola will be remembered as a friend to those searching for a better, richer life. In the precepts presented in *A Charlotte Mason Companion*, we find gentle encouragement and joy.

This book may be purchased directly through Charlotte Mason Research & Supply Co. PO Box 936, Elkton, MD 21922-0936.

The Religious Side of Education

In Charlotte Mason's day, faith in God was an accepted part of all education. Now only in private and home schools may anything religious be mentioned.

Jesus said to "Take heed that ye OFFEND not —DESPISE not — HINDER not —one of these little ones." (Vol. 1, p. 12)

Parents' highest function is as "revealers of God." (The second half of chap. VI is very good —deals with teaching children to pray and to know God. Vol. 2, Chap. V and VI)

Parents as Instructors in Religion — "Here we have the theory of the Sunday School —the parents who can, teach their children at home on Sunday, and substitutes step in to act for those who can not." (p. 92-93)

"Nothing should do more to strengthen the bonds of family life than that the children should learn religion at the lips of their parents..." (p. 94)

Parents as Teachers of Morals — "The Bible is not a single book, but a classic literature of wonderful beauty and interest... Here is poetry, the rhythm of which soothes even the jaded brain past taking pleasure in any other. Here is history, based on such broad, clear lines, such dealing of slow and sure and even handed justice to the nations, such stories of national sins and national repentances, the student realizes, as from no other history, the solidarity of the race, the brotherhood, and, if we may call it so, the individuality of the nations. Here is philosophy which, of all the philosophies that have been propounded, is alone adequate to the interpretation of human life. We say not a word here of that which is the *raison d'être* of the Bible, its teaching of religion, its revelation of God to man; but, to urge only one point more, all the literatures of the world put together utterly fail to give us a system of ethics, in precept and example, motive and sanction, complete as that to which we have been born as our common inheritance in the Bible." (p. 104)

"For 1700 years, roughly speaking, the Bible has been the school-book of modern Europe; its teaching, conveyed directly or indirectly, more or less pure, has been the basis upon which the whole superstructure of not only religious but ethical and, to some extent, literary training rested." (p. 104)

"It is a mistake to translate Bible stories into slipshod English, even when the narrator keeps close to the facts of the narrative. The rhythm and cadence of Biblical phraseology is as charming to a child as to his elders, if not more so. Read your Bible story to the child, bit by bit; get him to tell you in his own words (keeping as close as he can to the Bible words) what you have read, and then, if you like, talk about it; but not much." (p. 110)

"This is the faith in which we would bring up our children, this strong, passionate sense of the dear nearness of our God; firm in this conviction, the controversies of the day will interest but not exercise us, for we are on the other side of all doubt once we know Him in whom we have believed." (p. 135)

"Let mother never contemplate any kind of instruction for her child, except under the sense of divine co-operation." (p. 274)

"YE ARE NOT YOUR OWN. —But if children are brought up from the first with this magnet — 'Ye are *not* your own'; the divine Author of your being has given you life, and a body finely adapted for His service; He gives you the work of preserving this body in health, nourishing it in strength, and training it in fitness for whatever special work He may give you to do in His world, —why, young people themselves would readily embrace a more Spartan regimen... It would be good work to keep to the front this idea of living under authority, training under authority, serving under authority, a discipline of life readily self-embraced by children, in whom the heroic impulse is always strong. We would not reduce the pleasures of childhood and youth by an iota; rather we would increase them, for the disciplined life has more power of fresh enjoyment than is given to the unrestrained." (p. 103)

"PRINCIPLES, NOT RULES. — 'God does not allow' us to do thus and thus should be a rarely expressed but often present thought to parents who study the nature of the divine authority where it is most fully revealed, that is, in the Gospels." (p. 127)

"VALUE OF BIOGRAPHY. —The Bible is, of course, a storehouse of most inspiring biographies; but it would be well if we could manage our teaching so as to bring out in each character the master-thought of all his thinking." (p. 133)

"AUTHORITY IN RELIGIOUS EDUCATION. —A child cannot have a lasting sense of duty until he is brought into contact with a supreme Authority, who is the source of law, and the pleasing of whom converts duty into joy." (p. 137)

If children are willful and irreverent, it is because they "are brought up without the consciousness of their relation to God." (p. 138)

"THE HABIT OF READING THE BIBLE." Form the habit of listening to and reading scriptures —the actual scriptures. Children should be in the habit of praising God. Sing hymns. Keep the Sabbath holy. (p. 142)

"As for moral lessons, they are worse than useless; children want a great deal of fine and various moral feeding, from which they draw the 'lessons' they require... Trust, not to our own teaching, but to the best that we have in art and literature and above all to that storehouse of example and precept, the Bible, to enable us to touch these delicate spirits to fine issues." (Vol. 6, p. 59)

"But what sort of approaches do we prepare for children towards the God whom they need, the Savior in Whom is all help, the King Who affords all delight, commands all adoration and loyalty?

Any words or thoughts of ours are poor and insufficient, but we have a treasure of divine words that they read and know with satisfying pleasure and tell with singular beauty and fitness. 'The Bible is the most interesting book I know,' said a young person of ten who had read a good many books and knew her Bible." (p. 64)

"Of the three sorts of knowledge proper to a child, —the knowledge of God, of man, and of the universe, —the knowledge of God ranks first in importance, is indispensable, and most happy-making... We shall be astonished (if we don't talk down) at the range and depth of children's minds; and shall perceive that their relation to God is one of those 'first-born affinities' which it is our part to help them to make good." (p. 158)

"Now our objective in this most important part of education is to give the children the knowledge of God. We need not go into the question of intuitive knowledge, but the expressed knowledge attainable by us has its source in the Bible, and perhaps we cannot do a greater indignity to children than to substitute our own or some other benevolent person's rendering for the fine English, poetic diction and lucid statement of the Bible.

"Literature at its best is always direct and simple and a normal child of six listens with delight to the tales both of Old and New Testament read to him passage by passage, and by him narrated in turn, with delightful touches of native eloquence." (p. 160)

"Let us have faith and courage to give children such a full and gradual picture of Old Testament history that they unconsciously perceive for themselves a panoramic view of the history of mankind typified by that of the Jewish nation as it is unfolded in the Bible." (p. 162)

"The reverent reading of the text, with the following narration, is often curiously word perfect after a single reading; this is the more surprising because we all know how difficult it is to repeat a passage which we have heard a thousand times; the single attentive reading does away with this diffi-

culty and we are able to assure ourselves that children's minds are stored with perfect word pictures of every tender and beautiful scene described in the Gospels." (p. 165)

"Education is part and parcel of religion and every enthusiastic teacher knows that he is obeying the precept, — 'feed my lambs' —feed with all those things which are good and wholesome for the spirit of a man; and, before all and including all, with the knowledge of God." (p. 246)

"The knowledge of God is the principal knowledge, and no teaching of the Bible which does not further that knowledge is of religious value. Therefore the children read, or if they are too young to read for themselves the [parent] reads to them, a passage of varying length covering an incident or some definite teaching... The children narrate what has been read after the reading; they do this with curious accuracy and yet with some originality, conveying the spiritual teaching which the teacher has indicated. Now this is no parrot-exercise, but is the result of such an assimilation of the passage that it has become a part of the young scholar." (p. 272-273)

STUDY SUGGESTIONS: Vol. 1, Part IV, Chapter III; Vol. 2, Chapters X, XI; Vol. 3, Chapter XIII; Vol. 4, p.174 to end; Vol. 6, Chapter X

Charlotte Mason on the Three R's

Charlotte Mason gave us ideas on how to teach the basics. Especially novel and effective is her method of teaching spelling.

READING AND SPELLING

On learning the ABC's: "The learn-ing of the alphabet should be made a means of cultivating the child's observa-tion: he should be made to *see* what he looks at... To make the small letters from memory is a work of more art [than the capital letters], and requires more careful observation on the child's part. A tray of sand is useful... The child draws his finger boldly through the sand [to form the letter]... There is no occa-sion to hurry the child: let him learn one form at a time, and know it so well that he can pick out the *d's*, say, big and lit-tle, in a page of large print. Let him say  *d* for duck, dog, doll..." (p. 201; all quotes are from Vol. 1 unless other-wise indicated)

On phonics: Use magnetic letters to teach word families. Start with simple three letter combinations. When this becomes too easy, teach the long vowel words with a silent e at the end. Continue learning more complex phonics as the child is ready. (p. 202-203)

"EARLY SPELLING. —Accustom him from the first to shut his eyes and spell the word he has made. This is important. Reading is not spelling, nor is it necessary to spell in order to read well; but the good speller is the child whose eye is quick enough to take in the letters which compose it, in the act of reading off a word; and this is a habit to be acquired from the first: *accustom* him to *see* the letters in the word, and he will do so without effort." (p. 203-204)

"READING AT SIGHT." Take the first two lines of Twinkle. Print it on a sheet in large letters. Make another copy that is cut into word cards. Read the verse to the child while pointing to each word. Teach each word using the word cards. When he knows each word, "let him *read* the two lines with clear enunciation and expression: insist from the first on clear, beautiful reading, and do not let the child fall into a dreary monotone, no more pleasant to himself than to his listener." Then let him find these words he has just learned in a page of print. [You may want to use a computer to make your sheet since newsprint is so tiny and finding "twinkle" is doubtful.] "The child should hunt...for each of the words he has learned, until the word he knows looks out upon him like the face of a friend in a crowd of strangers, and he is able to pounce upon it anywhere." (p. 204-205)

"The next 'reading at sight' lesson will begin with a hunt for the familiar words, and then— "Up above the world so high, Like a diamond in the sky," should be gone through in the same way. As spelling is simply the art of *seeing,* seeing the letters in a word as we see the features of a face—say to the child, 'Can you spell sky?'—or any of the shorter words. He is put on his mettle, and if he fail this time, be sure he will be able to spell the word when you ask him next..." (p. 205)

He should master about ten new words a day and review the ones already learned. Learn to spell as you go along. Remember to spell by closing eyes and seeing the whole word in your mind. Enunciate—di-a-mond, not di'mond. In the usual method, the child is stumbling, guessing, blundering his way through the lesson in a monotone. Using Miss Mason's method, the child is establishing that habit of perfect execution of which she said, "No work should be given to a child that he cannot execute *perfectly,* and then perfection should be required of him as a matter of course..." (p. 159)

"Learning to read is no more than picking up, how we can, a knowledge of certain arbitrary symbols for objects and ideas... What we want is a bridge between the child's natural interests and those arbitrary symbols with which he must become acquainted, and which, as we have seen, are words, and not letters... But the thing he learns to know by looking at it, is a thing which interests him. Here we have the key to reading. No meaningless combinations of letters...should be presented to him. The child should be taught from the first to regard the printed word as he already regards the spoken word, as the symbol of fact or idea full of interest. How easy to read 'robin redbreast,' buttercups and daisies'; the number of letters in the words does not matter; the words themselves convey such interesting ideas that the general form and look of them fixes itself on the child's brain by the same law of association of ideas which makes it easy to couple the objects with their spoken names. Having got a word fixed on the sure peg of the idea it conveys, the child will use his knowledge of the sounds of the letters to make up other words containing the same elements with great interest. When he knows 'butter' he is quite ready to make 'mutter' by changing the *b* for an *m*." (p. 215-216)

"TOMMY'S FIRST LESSON ...This is the sort of reading lesson we have in view. Tommy knows his letters by name and sound, but he knows no more. Today he is to be launched into the very middle of reading, without any 'steps' at all, because reading is neither an art nor a science, and has, probably, no beginning. Tommy is to learn to read today— "I like little pussy, Her coat is so warm" —and he is to know those nine words so well that he will be able to read them wherever they may occur henceforth and forevermore."

Make the word cards. Have magnetic letters handy. Write the word pussy on paper or chalkboard. Tell him what the word is. "Interest at once; he knows the thing, pussy, and the written symbol is pleasant in his eyes because it is associated with an existing idea in his mind. He is told to look at the word 'pussy' until he is sure he would know it again. Then he makes 'pussy' from memory with his own loose letter. [The word cards] are turned out, and he finds the word 'pussy'; and lastly, the little sheet with the poem printed on it is shown to him, and he finds 'pussy,' but is not allowed yet to find out the run of the rhyme. 'Coat, little, like, is, her, warm, I, so,' are taught in the same way, in less time than it takes to describe the lesson...

"READING SENTENCES. —He knows words now, but he cannot yet read sentences. Now for the delight of *reading*. He finds at our dictation, amongst his loose words, 'pussy-is-warm,' places them in 'reading' order, one after the other, and then reads off the sentence. Joy, as of one who has found a new planet! And Tommy has indeed found a new power. Then, 'her-little-coat-is-warm,' 'Pussy-is-so-little,' 'I-like-pussy,' 'Pussy-is-little-like-her-coat,' and so on through a dozen more little arrangements. If the rhyme can be kept a secret till the whole is worked out, so much the better. To make the verses up with his own loose words [word cards] will give Tommy such a delicious sense that knowledge is power, as few occasions in after life will afford. Anyway, reading is to him a delight henceforth.

"TOMMY'S SECOND LESSON. —Tommy promises himself another reading lesson next day, but he has instead a spelling lesson...He makes the word 'coat' with his letter, from memory if he can; if not, with the pattern word. Say 'coat' slowly; give the sound of the c. 'Take away c, and what have we left?' A little help will get 'oat' from him. How would you make 'boat'?... float, goat, moat... Tommy will, no doubt, offer 'note,' and we must make a clean breast of it and say, 'No, *note* is spelt with other letters'; but what other letters we do not tell him now." Write all the new words he has formed on cards. Dictate to him some sentences using the new words and have him arrange the word cards into these sentences. In the next lesson, follow these same steps of forming new words from the other known words. And forming real sentences with all these words. In following lessons, continue learning the words to the rest of the rhyme. (p. 217-221)

"Unknown Words. —Now for a new experience. We dictate 'pussy is in the boat.' Consternation! Tommy does not know 'in' nor 'the.' 'Put counters for the words you don't know; they may soon come in our lessons,' and Tommy has a desire and a need—that is, an appetite for learning." (p. 220)

"MORAL TRAINING IN READING LESSONS ...By the time Tommy has worked 'Little Pussy' through he has quite a large stock of words; has considerable power to attack new words with familiar combinations; what is more, he has achieved; he has courage to attack all 'learning,' and has a sense that delightful results are quite within reach. Moreover, he learns to read in a way that affords him some moral training. There is no stumbling, no hesitation from the first, but bright attention and perfect achievement. His reading lesson is a delight, of which he is deprived when he comes to his lesson in a lazy, drawling mood. Perfect enunciation and precision are insisted on, and when he comes to arrange the whole of the little rhyme in his loose words and read it off (most delightful of all the lessons) his reading must be a perfect and finished recitation." (p. 221-222)

"The child who has been taught to read with care and deliberation until he has mastered the words of a limited vocabulary, usually does the rest for himself. The attention of his teachers should be fixed on two points—that he acquires the *habit* of reading, and that he does not fall into *slipshod habits* of reading." (p. 226)

"THE RATIONALE OF SPELLING. —But the fact is, the gift of spelling depends upon the power the eye possesses to 'take' (in a photographic sense) a detailed picture of a word; and this is a power and habit which must be cultivated in children from the first. When they have read 'cat,' they must be encouraged to see the word with their eyes shut, and the same habit will enable them to image 'Thermopylae.' This picturing of words upon the retina appears to me to be the only royal road to spelling; an error once made and corrected leads to fearful doubt for the rest of one's life, as to which was the wrong way and which the right... It becomes, therefore, the teacher's business to prevent false spelling, and if an error has been made, to hide it away, as it were, so that the impression may not become fixed." (p. 241)

"The whole secret of spelling lies in the habit of visualizing words from memory, and children must be trained to visualize in the course of their reading. They enjoy this way of learning to spell." (p. 243)

HANDWRITING AND COMPOSITION

"First, let the child accomplish something *perfectly* in every lesson... Let the writing lesson be short; it should not last more than five or ten minutes... The thing to be avoided is the habit of careless work." Sort the  letters into families of similarly formed letters. Learn one letter a day perfectly. "Secure that the child *begins* by making perfect letters and is never allowed to make faulty ones, and the rest he will do for himself." Later the child should copy one line as perfectly as possible, even if he must write it several times to get the one perfect copy. (p. 233-235)

Children should not be taught composition; narration leads naturally to composition. "Lessons on 'composition' should follow the model of that famous essay on 'Snakes in Ireland'- 'There are none.'...Children who have been in the habit of using books will write good, vigorous English with ease and freedom; that is, if they have not been hampered by instructions... Our business is to provide children with material in their lessons, and, leave the handling of such material to themselves. If we would believe it, composition is as natural as jumping and running to children who have been allowed due use of books. They should narrate in the first place, and they will compose, later, readily enough; but they should not be taught 'composition.'" (p. 247)

"...All their work lends itself to oral composition and the power of such composition is innate in children and is not the result of instruction." (Vol. 6, p. 191)

"Composition is not an adjunct but an integral part of their education in every subject." (Vol. 6, p. 192)

ARITHMETIC

"The chief value of arithmetic, like that of the higher mathematics, lies in the training it affords to the reasoning powers, and in the habits of insight, readiness, accuracy, intellectual truthfulness it engenders... Multiplication does not produce the 'right answer,' so the boy tries division; that again fails, but subtraction may get him out of the bog. There is no *must be* to him; he does not see that one process, and one process *only*, can give the required result. Now, a child who does not know what rule to apply to a simple problem within his grasp has been ill taught from the first, although he may produce slatefuls of quite right sums in multiplication or long division." (p. 254)

Use word problems so the child must figure out for himself which operation to use. "Say to him, 'Mr. Jones sent six hundred and seven and Mr. Stevens eight hundred and nineteen, apples to be divided amongst the twenty-seven boys at school on Monday. How many apples apiece did they get?

"Here he must ask himself certain questions. 'How many apples altogether? How shall I find out? Then I must *divide* the apples into twenty-seven heaps to find out each boy's share.' That is to say, the child perceives what rules he must apply to get the required information. He is interested; the work goes on briskly: the sum is done in no time, and is probably right, because the attention of the child is concentrated on his work. Care must be taken to give the child such problems as he *can* work, but yet which are difficult enough to cause him some little mental effort." (p. 255)

Use manipulatives to demonstrate the reasoning. To teach place value, use pennies and dimes, and then dollars. Give the child many opportunities to estimate, and then to weigh and measure to see how closely he can guess.

"Mathematics depend upon the teacher rather than upon the text-book and few subjects are worse taught; chiefly because teachers have seldom time to give the inspiring ideas...which should quicken imagination. How living would Geometry become in the light of the discoveries of Euclid as he made them! To sum up, Mathematics are a necessary part of every man's education; they must be taught by those who know; but they may not engross the time and attention of the scholar in such wise as to shut out any of the score of 'subjects,' a knowledge of which is his natural rights." (Vol. 6, p. 233)

Thought: What if we taught math facts the way that Charlotte said to teach spelling? Give the child a fact card with the answer. Let him demonstrate it with manipulatives. Cover one part of the equation and ask him to tell the missing number. Ask him to tell the fact to you when he sees it in his mind. Wouldn't this work? It's worth a try at least with those troublesome facts.

STUDY SUGGESTIONS: Vol. 1, Part V, chapters 4-15

The Royal Road to Spelling

We all make mistakes along this journey of home education. Sometimes the road we choose seems right but leads nowhere. But what a good education to parents these mistakes can be! Years ago with my first child, I let her use invented spelling as long as it made sense phonetically. I had heard that given time and lots of reading, a child would naturally become a good speller. When a ten-year-old, who has long been an avid reader, still spells 'said' as 'sed,' you realize you've made a big mistake!

I have used only Charlotte Mason's method of spelling with my eight-year-old son and I'm totally amazed at the results. This method really works! My ten-year-old son is not as good with it, probably because he did not start with this method. But he is becoming accustomed to it and his spelling is improving.

Charlotte wrote, "Early Spelling. —Accustom him from the first to shut his eyes and spell the word he has made. This is important. Reading is not spelling, nor is it necessary to spell in order to read well; but the good speller is the child whose eye is quick enough to take in the letters which compose it, in the act of reading off a word; and this is a habit to be acquired from the first; accustom him to see the letters in the word, and he will do so without effort." (Vol. 1, p. 203-204) I believe that this is what Miss Mason was referring to when she said children would naturally become better spellers. First they had been trained in this habit of really seeing the letters in a word —of visualizing the spelling. This habit, once fully formed, made correct spelling a natural by-product of reading.

Let your child spell simple, phonetic words by sounding them out. But use Charlotte's method to teach the spelling of more complex words and irregular words. I started out showing a short irregular word on a card to my son. (Some good words to start with: said, has, is, are, come, the.) When he felt he

had a picture of the word in his mind, I would turn the card over and he would spell it from memory. If he made a mistake, I would immediately show him the word again so he would not have the wrong spelling in his mind. The child can say the letters of the word, or arrange magnetic letters to form it, or write the word out. Use whichever works best for him or enjoy variety by using a different method each day.

We usually do something a bit different, now that Logan is comfortable with this spelling method. Immediately, after he reads to me, I choose a word from his actual reading. He tells me if he needs to look at it before attempting to spell it. If the word was 'show,' I might ask him to spell 'blow' and 'snow' after he correctly spelled the word from his reading. I believe taking the spelling words from that day's reading really helps "accustom him to see the letters in the word" as he is reading. This habit of visualizing a word is the true key to good spelling.

Charlotte explained of spelling: "But the fact is, the gift of spelling depends upon the power the eye possesses to 'take' (in a photographic sense) a detailed picture of a word; and this is a power and habit which must be cultivated in children from the first. When they have read 'cat,' they must be encouraged to see the word with their eyes shut, and the same habit will enable them to image 'Thermopylae.' This picturing of words upon the retina appears to me to be the only royal road to spelling; an error once made and corrected leads to fearful doubt for the rest of one's life, as to which was the wrong way and which the right... It becomes, therefore, the teacher's business to prevent false spelling, and if an error has been made, to hide it away, as it were, so that the impression may not become fixed." (Vol. 1, p. 241)

How many words cause us problems? We've spelled them wrong so many times that we never can remember which way is correct. Even when we write it out two or three ways, we're not sure which way is right. Using Miss Mason's advice, we try to never let children spell words incorrectly. We hurry and erase it (or white it out) so the wrong visual image is not set in the child's mind.

We want to establish the habit of perfect spelling from the beginning —the habit of taking a mental photograph of the word. Avoid my mistake on your journey of educating your children by following this 'royal road' to good spelling.

The Telling Road to Writing

Which road will lead us to producing children who are good writers? Forcing children to write everyday may instill a life-long aversion to any writing. Never requiring writing may result in a child who can't write because he never has written. I believe that daily oral narration or retelling is the best road to composition—to a child who can write well. Narration may be thought of as composition. Those compositions may be oral or written. For most children under ten, it is best to stick to oral narrations. We can just listen to the telling. We may record narrations onto a cassette tape or on paper.

Expect the transition from oral to written narrations to be gradual. Ten or eleven-year-olds may take a couple of years before they are ready to write independently. Perhaps they'll write the first part and ask to dictate the rest of the composition. Even after children are independent writers, continue asking for oral narrations regularly. This really improves their public speaking skills.

Instead of worrying about which writing/language arts curriculum materials to use, we simply let our children retell, in their own words, something they've read or listened to. What a natural, easy way to get kids to write! There's no need for lesson plans or preparation. There's no cost involved. Charlotte Mason said that composition should not be taught; narration leads naturally to composition.

Use "living" books as sources for narration. This means we read the best written, most uplifting, inspiring works we can find. By narrating from the best books, our children are gleaning from some of the best literary styles. One mother said her daughter's writing skills improved as they read a good quality novel. Her daughter was inspired to use more

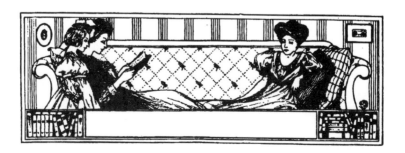

description in her stories. Children will develop their own style after a few years of reading and retelling from master storytellers.

Students may keep a notebook of all the good literature they've read. They may wish to include one or more quotes from each book—a thought that particularly struck them. This notebook could be part of the student's portfolio for college entrance. Their narrations of classics and other good literature could also be saved in a portfolio.

We should not repeat readings. When children are aware of the "certainty" of being asked to retell, they will attend better. My personal experience can verify this. At a home education convention workshop, the instructor read a passage to us. Then he surprised us by asking us to write ten facts. I couldn't recall more than three or four. The next time I attended another of this instructor's workshops, you can bet I paid more attention to the reading! I knew the certainty of what would be requested.

What would our minds be capable of, if we had been educated in this fashion? Where would our writing skills be? Our children will probably astound us with their efforts if we have the courage to educate them as Miss Mason proposed. We have the opportunity to let them reach their full potential as they travel the telling road to writing.

Geography and History

Before Miss Mason wrote *Home Education,* she wrote a series of successful geography books. Her love of geography and history shines through in these quotes.

"The peculiar value of geography lies in its fitness to nourish the mind with ideas, and to furnish the imagination with pictures. Herein lies the educational value of geography." (Vol. 1, p. 272)

Geography, as usually taught, "has never been really received by the brain at all... For *educative* purposes, the child must learn such geography, and in such a way, that his mind shall thereby be stored with ideas, his imagination with images; for *practical* purposes he must learn such geography only as, the nature of his mind considered, he will be able to remember; in other words, he must learn what *interests* him. (p. 273)

"The child gets his rudimentary notions of geography...in those long hours out of door... He gets his first notions of a map from a rude sketch...or with a stick in the sand or gravel." (p. 273-274)

"Let him be *at home* in any single region; let him see, with the mind's eye, the people at their work and at their play, the flowers and fruits in their seasons, the beasts, each in its habitat; and let him see all *sympathetically,* that is, let him follow the adventures of a traveler; and he knows more, is better furnished with ideas, than if he had learnt all the names on all the maps. The 'way' of this kind of teaching is very simple and obvious; read to him...bit by bit...any interesting, well-written book of travel. It may be necessary to leave out a good deal, but every illustrative anecdote, every bit of description, is so much towards the child's education. Here, as elsewhere, the question is, not how many things does he know, but how *much* does he know about each thing." (p. 275)

"A sketch-map following the traveler's progress [is] compared finally with a complete map of the region... In the course of his readings he falls in with a description of a volcano, a glacier, a canyon, a hurricane; he hears all about, and asks and learns the how and the why, of such phenomena at the moment when his interest is excited. In other words, he learns as his elders elect to learn for themselves, though they rarely allow the children to tread in paths so pleasant." (p. 275-276)

"The fatal mistake is in the notion that he must learn 'outlines,' of the *whole* history...just as he must cover the geography of *all* the world. Let him, on the contrary, linger pleasantly over the history of a single man, a short period, until he thinks the thoughts of that man, is at home in the ways of that period. Though he is reading and thinking of the lifetime of a single man, he is really getting intimately acquainted with the history of a whole nation for a whole age." (p. 280)

Have the child create his own timeline. "Let the child himself write, or print, as he is able, the names of the people he comes upon in due order, in their proper century. We need not trouble ourselves at present with more exact dates, but this simple table of the centuries will suggest a graphic panorama to the child's mind, and he will see events in their time-order."(p. 292)

"History readings afford admirable material for narration, and children enjoy narrating what they have read or heard. They love, too, to make illustrations." (p. 292)

"Children have other ways of expressing the conceptions that fill them when they are duly fed. They play at their history lessons, dress up, make tableaux, act scenes; or they have a stage, and the dolls act, while they paint the scenery and speak the speeches. There is no end to the modes of expression children find when there is anything in them to express.

"The mistake we make is to suppose that imagination is fed by nature, or that it works on the insipid diet of children's story-books. Let a child have the meat he requires in his history readings, and in the literature which naturally gathers round this history, and imagination will bestir itself without any help of ours; the child will live out in detail a thousand scenes of which he only gets the merest hint." (p. 294-295)

STUDY SUGGESTIONS: Vol. 1, Part 5, Chapters 17 and 18; Vol. 6, p. 169-180 and p. 224-230

Living Books for Living Children

Charlotte Mason urged us to use living books as our core curriculum. "...We owe it to every child to put him in communication with great minds that he may get at great thoughts; with the minds, that is of those who have left us great works; and the only vital method of education appears to be that children should read worthy books, many worthy books." (Vol. 6, p. 12)

I like the following definition of a living book that a reader sent into "Parent's Review," Winter 1994. Vicki Surbatovich wrote, "To me, a living book is a book so well-done, the story so smoothly flowing, the passions so nobly excited, the mind and morals so well-nourished, that we are better people (not merely better informed) than if we had not read the book." Living books present information and ideas in a conversational way. They are very well written and are worth remembering.

To start implementing narration, choose a fairly short book that is written in a style your children can relate to. It's important to have a good first experience with the read-aloud followed by narration formula. Here are a few possibilities for those with young children (elementary grades) or for those just beginning a read-aloud program: *The Thanksgiving Story, The Courage of Sarah Noble, The Bears on Hemlock Mountain* by Alice Dalgliesh; *The Cabin Faced West* by Jean Fritz; *Just So Stories* by Rudyard Kipling; *The Light at Tern Rock* by Julia Sauer (an uplifting, Santa-less Christmas story); *Aesop's Fables; The Hundred Dresses* by Eleanor Estes; *The Sword in the Tree, A Lion to Guard Us, The Wish at the Top* by Clyde Robert Bulla; *My Father's Dragon* (and others in the trilogy) by Ruth Stiles Gannett.

Studying history following

Charlotte Mason's principles makes perfect sense. What better way to internalize and retain history than by narrating from living books? You could thoroughly study one period. Or you could read an overview of history and supplement along the way with biographies and historical fiction. *A Child's History of the World* by V. M. Hillyer is a good overview for elementary aged students. *The Light and the Glory* and *From Sea to Shining Sea* by Peter Marshall and David Manuel could be read as the stories fit into the time frame being studied. Readings from *The Book of Virtues* by William Bennett may also be correlated into the history outline. *Margaret Pumphrey's Pilgrim Stories* make for good narrations. For junior and senior high school levels, my favorite for American history is Clarence Carson's five-volume set *A Basic History of the United States.*

In our family, each child creates his own history notebook. These include a timeline, drawings, mazes, puzzles, and other items that correlate with the time period. Most importantly, the student's narrations, from the historical material read, are kept in the notebook. My kids listen better if they are occupied with a coloring sheet related to the lesson for the day. They take great pride in these history notebooks and beg to continue if we take a break from working in them.

Learning history through the lives of individuals is recognized by many as an excellent method. Older students might try *The Real George Washington* (and others in the series) published by the National Center for Constitutional Studies or the Sower Series.

Some biographies for the younger set that we've enjoyed are: *Benjamin West and His Cat, Grimalkin* by Marguerite Henry; *Millet Tilled the Soil* by Sybil Deucher and Opal Wheeler; *Louis Braille, The Boy Who Invented Books for the Blind* by Margaret Davidson; *Squanto, Friend of the Pilgrims* by Clyde Robert Bulla; *The Apple and the Arrow*

by Mary and Conrad Buff.

Historical fiction boasts many living books that are well worth reading. Their supplemental value is immense because they bring history alive. Young students will enjoy *The Matchlock Gun* by Walter Edmonds and *Phoebe the Spy* by Judith

Berry Griffin. The following books are for older children (upper elementary through high school): *The Door in the Wall* by Marguerite de Angeli; *Johnny Tremain* by Esther Forbes; *Calico Bush* by Rachel Field; *The Trumpeter of Krakow* by Eric Kelly; *Carry On, Mr. Bowditch* by Jean Lee Latham; *Moccasin Trail and The Golden Goblet* by Eloise Jarvis McGraw; *Caddie Woodlawn* by Carol Ryrie Brink; *The Defender* by Nicholas Kalashnikoff; *Sarah Bishop* by Scott O'Dell; *The Bronze Bow, The Sign of the Beaver,* and *The Witch of Blackbird Pond* by Elizabeth George Speare.

Shakespeare, poetry, and the classics should also be a part of the curriculum. *Tales from Shakespeare* by Charles and Mary Lamb might be the best way to start elementary age children on Shakespeare. The greatest living book ever written is *The Holy Bible.* It is literature and history at their best —and much more. Narrating from its passages could be the most fulfilling part of the curriculum.

Fairy tales by Andersen and the Brothers Grimm and *Tales from the Arabian Nights* could be enjoyed. We should also introduce our children to Greek and Roman myths and tales. As a fan of fantasy, I also recommend these books: *A Wrinkle in Time* (and others in this series) by Madeleine L'Engle; *The Hobbit, The Lord of the Rings Trilogy* by J. R. R. Tolkien; *The Chronicles of Narnia* by C. S. Lewis; *At the Back of the North Wind* by George MacDonald; *Winter of Fire* by Sherryl Jordan.

For a more complete listing of living books check the anthologies found in the library. Charlotte Mason said, "The best thought the world possesses is stored in books; we must open books to children, the best books." May we search and introduce our children to living books. Narrating from living books will store treasures up in the minds of our children forever.

The Arts

Charlotte Mason was a lover of all the arts. During vacations she would visit museums in Europe. She read and wrote much poetry. Along with her associates, she developed ways of helping children establish relationships with the arts.

MUSIC APPRECIATION

"THE HABIT OF MUSIC. —As for musical training, it would be hard to say how much that passes for inherited musical taste and ability is the result of the constant hearing and producing of musical sounds, the *habit* of music, that the child of musical people grows up with... The art of singing is entirely a trained habit...every child may be, and should be, trained to sing. Of course, *transmitted* habit must be taken into account. It is a pity that the musical training most children get is of a random character; that they are not trained, for instance, by carefully graduated ear and voice exercises, to produce and distinguish musical tones and intervals." (Vol. 1, p. 133)

"I should like, in connection with singing, to mention the admirable educational effects of the Tonic Sol-fa method. Children learn by it in a magical way to produce sign for sound and sound for sign, that is, they can not only read music, but can write the notes for, or make the proper hand signs for, the notes of a passage sung to them. Ear and voice are simultaneously and equally cultivated." ... Look for a piano method which is "worked out, with minute care, upon the same lines; that is, the child's knowledge of the theory of music and his ear training keep pace with his power of execution, and seem to do away with the deadly dreariness of 'practicing.'" (Vol. 1, p.314-315)

"MUSIC, THE GREAT JOY WE OWE TO HEARING. —Hearing should tell us a great many interesting things, but the great and perfect joy which we owe to him is *Music*. Many great men have put their beautiful thoughts, not into books, or pictures, or buildings, but into musical score, to be sung with the voice or played on instruments, and so full are these musical compositions of the minds of their makers, that people who care for music can always tell who has composed the music they hear, even if they have never heard the particular movement before. Thus, in a manner, the composer speaks to them, and they are perfectly happy in listening to what he has to say. Quite little children can sometimes get a good deal of this power; indeed, I knew a boy of three years old who knew when his mother was playing 'Wagner,' for example. She played to him a great deal, and he *listened.* Some people have more power in this way than others, but we might all have far more than we possess if we listened." (Vol. 4, p. 30-31)

Charlotte quoted Mrs. Glover who gave a talk at an Ambleside Conference in 1922: "Musical Appreciation—which is so much before the eye at the present moment—originated in the P.N.E.U. about twenty-five years ago. At that time I was playing to my little child much of the best music in which I was interested, and Miss Mason happened to hear of what I was doing. She realized that music might give great joy and interest to the life of all, and she felt that just as children in the P.U.S. were given the greatest literature and art, so they should have the greatest music as well. She asked me to write an article in the *Review* on the result of my observations, and to make a program of music each term that might be played to the children. From that day to this, at the beginning of every term a program has appeared; thus began a movement that was to spread far and wide.

"Musical Appreciation, of course, has nothing to do with playing the piano. It used to be thought that 'learning music' must mean this, and it was supposed that children who had no talent for playing were unmusical and would not like concerts. But Musical Appreciation had no more to do with playing an instrument than acting had to do with an appreciation of Shakespeare, or painting with enjoyment of pictures. I think that all children should take Musical Appreciation and not only the musical ones, for it has been proved that only three per cent of children are what is called 'tone-deaf'; and if they are taken at an early age it is astonishing how children who appear to be without ear, develop it and are able to enjoy listening to music with understanding." (Vol. 6, p. 217-218)

"We are perceiving, too, that a human being is endowed with an ear attuned to harmony and melody, with a voice from which music may issue, hands whose delicate action may draw forth sounds in enthralling sequence. With the ancient Greeks, we begin to realize that music is a necessary part of education." (Vol. 6, p. 329)

ART APPRECIATION

"The art training of children should proceed on two lines. The six-year-old child should begin both to express himself and to appreciate, and his appreciation should be well in advance of his power to express what he sees or images." (Vol. 1, p. 306)

"The study of pictures should not be left to chance, but they should take one artist after another, term by term, and study quietly some half-dozen reproductions of his work in the course of a term... We cannot measure the influence that one or another artist has upon the child's sense of beauty, upon his power of seeing, as in a picture, the common sight of life; he is enriched more than we know in having really looked at even a single picture." (p. 309)

"We attach a good deal of value to what we call picture talks, that is: —a reproduction of a suitable picture, by Millet, for example, is put into the children's hands, and they study it by themselves. Then, children of from six to nine describe the picture, giving all the details and showing by a few lines where is such a tree or such a house; judging if they can the time of day; discovering the story if there be one. The older children add to this some study of the lines of composition, light and shade, the particular style of the master; and reproduce from memory certain details. The object of these lessons is that the pupils should learn how to appreciate rather than how to produce." (Vol. 3, p. 239)

"There are always those present with us whom God whispers in the ear, through whom He sends a direct message to the rest. Among these messengers are the great painters who interpret to us some of the meanings of life. To read their messages aright is a thing due from us. But this, like other good gifts, does not come by nature. It is the reward of humble, patient study. It is not in a day or a year that Fra Angelico will tell us of the beauty of holiness, that Giotto will confide his interpretation of the meaning of life, that Millet will tell us of the simplicity and dignity that belong to labor on the soil, that Rembrandt will show us the sweetness of humanity in many a commonplace countenance." (Vol. 4, p. 102)

"That we may be in a condition to receive this grace of teaching from all great Art, we must learn to appreciate and to discriminate, to separate between the meretricious and the essential, between technique (the mere power of expression) and the thing to be expressed—though the thing be no more than the grace and majesty of a tree. [This is] a debt we owe, and a debt we must acquire the means to pay by patient and humble study. In this, as in all the labors of the conscience seeking for instruction, we are enriched by our efforts; but self-culture should not be our object. Let us approach Art with the modest intention to pay a debt that we owe in learning to appreciate." (p. 103)

"Children should learn pictures, line by line, group by group, by reading, not books, but pictures themselves. A friendly picture-dealer supplies us with half a dozen beautiful reproductions of the work of some single artist, term by term. After a short story of the artist's life...the pictures are studied one at a time. Children learn not merely to see a picture but *to look at it,* taking in every detail. Then the picture is turned over and the children tell what they have seen... In this way children become acquainted with a hundred great artists during their school-life and it is an intimacy which never forsakes them." (Vol. 6, p. 214-215)

"There is no talk about schools of painting, little about style; consideration of these matters comes in later life [around 14], but the first and most important thing is to know the pictures themselves. As in a worthy book we leave the author to tell his own tale, so do we trust a picture to tell its tale through the medium the artist gave it.

In the region of art as elsewhere we shut out the middleman." (p. 216)

"With the ancient Greeks, we begin to realize that music is a necessary part of education. So, too, of pictorial art; at last we understand that every one can draw, and that, because to draw is delightful, every one should be taught how; that every one delights in pictures, and that education is concerned to teach him what pictures to delight in." (p. 329)

POETRY AND RECITATION

"All children have it in them to recite; it is an imprisoned gift waiting to be delivered, like Ariel from the pine... The child should speak beautiful thoughts so beautifully, with such delicate rendering of each *nuance* of meaning, that he becomes to the listener the interpreter of the author's thought." (Vol. 1, p. 223)

"I hope that my readers will train their children in the art of recitation; in the coming days, more even than in our own, will it behoove every educated man and woman to be able to speak effectively in public; and, in learning to recite you learn to speak." (p. 224)

"A thousand thoughts that burn come to us on the wings of verse; and, conceive how our lives would be impoverished were we to awake one day and find that the Psalms had disappeared from the world and from the thoughts of men! Proverbs, too, the words of the wise king and the sayings of the common folk, come to us as if they were auguries..." (Vol. 4, Book II, p. 11)

"Poetry is, perhaps, the most searching and intimate of our teachers... Poetry supplies us with tools for the modeling of our lives, and the use of these we must get at for ourselves... What we digest we assimilate, take into ourselves, so that it is part and parcel of us, and no longer separable." (p. 71-72)

"...The best thoughts of the best minds taking form as literature, and at its highest as poetry, or as poetry rendered in the plastic forms of art." (Vol. 6, p. 157)

STUDY SUGGESTIONS: Vol. 1, Part III, Chapter IX; Part V, Chapters VII, XXI; Vol. 4, Book II, Chapters II, XII, XV; Vol. 6, p. 213-217

"Dreaming of Dancing" drawn by April Gardner, at age 12

Art Appreciation Notebook

That's an intimidating title for us culturally deprived parents who have never been exposed to any form of Art Appreciation! But don't be scared off. This rewarding hobby or enrichment project can take as little as five minutes a week. It may be accomplished with little cost. Here are some ideas to get your notebook started.

PICTURE STUDY

Charlotte Mason called this subject "Picture Study." She recommended studying one artist at a time so children can become aware of that artist's style and can recognize his works even when a particular painting was not studied. Six works the artist should be studied; you could spend three or four weeks (once a week for five-ten minutes) on each work.

You may first want to introduce the artist. Tell enough about the artist to get the kids familiar with him, avoiding inappropriate personal details where necessary. Sometimes you can find a picture book or a short biographical story about the artist that you have chosen. Ask for a narration about the artist, after the reading, to include in the notebook.

During picture study sessions, let the children quietly look at the picture. After they've had a couple of minutes to take it in, turn the picture

over and ask for a narration. Older students may write their own narration in another room while you take dictation from the younger ones. You'll be amazed at the details children pick up —at their power of observation. Here is the first attempt at picture study narration from my two oldest children. Remember that these are told from memory with the picture out of sight.

Renoir's "A Girl With a Watering Can"
by April Gardner, age 10

It's a picture of a girl. She has a blue dress on with lace and buttons all down her dress. She's holding a watering can in one hand and two flowers in the other. There's a rose bush on the side of her and lots of flowers in the background. She's standing on a sidewalk. Her blonde hair is held up with a red ribbon. She has blue eyes and black boots.

Millet's "Angelus"
by Colton Gardner, age 8

There's a man and a lady praying. The man was wearing jeans and a leather vest and a white shirt underneath and wooden shoes. The lady was wearing an apron, wooden shoes and a bonnet. A basket of brown potatoes and a rake is behind the man stuck in the ground. They were standing on some dirt. And there was a town in the background. In the background was houses and a church.

In another picture study session, let the child look at the same picture again. Turn the picture over, after a couple minutes, and ask for a sketch of the painting. The third week, you might ask the child to make up an imaginative story that could possibly be behind the picture. For the last week, you might give the kids a choice of giving a verbal or a pictorial narration of the same painting after studying it anew. Place narrations and sketches in the notebook you are creating.

Repeat this process for each of the half dozen works of your chosen artist. To conclude the unit, ask each child for a narration of his or her favorite picture of those just studied. Why was it his favorite? This final narration may be even more detailed than the original one. Of course, this narration should also go in the notebook.

ART NOTEBOOK

The family art appreciation notebook or portfolio is a joy to create and a cherished keepsake. You may choose to use a three-prong report cover for each individual artist. Or you could use a three-ring binder with a divider separating each new artist as studied and added to your collection. Since this may become a favorite for browsing, you might consider inserting pictures and written material into plastic sheet protectors for durability.

Locate poems that correlate with the paintings studied. These greatly enhance the notebook and may even be memorized. Include original poetry, if a family member is inspired to produce something. Listen to music from the era of the artist. Perhaps even read a book that was written about the same time as the picture was painted. What was happening in the artist's country at that time?

Sometimes it is difficult to find six works of one artist. In the Millet section of our portfolio, we have only three prints. We found another one in a library book, so we were two short of Miss Mason's recommendation. With other artists this is not a problem. An inexpensive way to study art is using a book from the library. Then you have a good-sized picture to look at. It is best to borrow a book containing just the works of your chosen artist.

In our notebook, pasted below the narration of "A Girl With a Watering Can" is a tiny 1" x 1 1/2" color picture. This combined with the narration is enough to recall the large 10" x 14" reproduction studied. You can get reproductions of many paintings through: Publications Sales, National Gallery of Art, Washington, D.C. 20565. Another source is: Art Extension Press, Box 389, Westport, CN 06881.

We have also used calendar prints. If the picture is too large to fit in our notebook, we paste the small picture from the back of the calendar into our notebook. Some people use postcard-size prints. These are great for the notebook but you will still get more detail by studying a large reproduction from a coffee table book or large library book.

WORTHWHILE ENDEAVOR

Charlotte Mason felt an important part of one's education is getting intimately acquainted with great art. In her words, "Children should learn pictures, line by line, group by group, by reading, not books, but pictures themselves. A friendly picture-dealer supplies us with half a dozen beautiful reproductions of the work of some single artist, term by term. After a short story of the artist's life...the pictures are studied one at a time. Children learn not merely to see a picture but *to look at it,* taking in every detail. Then the picture is turned over and the children tell what they have seen. In this way children become acquainted with a hundred great artists during their school-life and it is an intimacy which never forsakes them... There is no talk about schools of painting, little about style; consideration of these matters comes in later life, [around 14] but the first and most important thing is to know the pictures themselves." (Vol. 6, p. 213-217)

A music critic once wrote: "Here is Tchaikovsky at his best. Music so beautiful it has to be heard to be appreciated." So it is with art; it has to be *seen* to be appreciated. This natural, unassuming approach to art appreciation seems so right. We don't want to become art critics, but art lovers. And we should never come between our children and the art they are observing.

We may wonder if we can squeeze one more thing into a busy schedule, but these few minutes once a week may be some of the most rewarding time spent. Creating a family art appreciation notebook is a worthwhile endeavor. Approach it as a fun family hobby, not a chore. Feel good about what you accomplish even if it falls short of your goal. Miss Mason said, "We cannot measure the influence that one or another artist has upon the child's sense of beauty, upon his power of seeing, as in a picture, the common sight of life; he is enriched more than we know in having really looked at even a single picture." Karen Andreola wrote in today's *Parents' Review,* "Just as Literature introduces us to the thought of the greatest writers, so Picture Study opens the gates to the ideas of the famous artists." This is a special way to enrich the lives of our children and ourselves.

Reciting: An Old-Fashioned Art

When I was a child in rural Vermont, I walked the dirt road a quarter of a mile to wait at "the little red schoolhouse" for the bus to pick me up. Both of my grandmothers taught school in that very building so that it had a lot of meaning for me. The first room was a kind of cloakroom with a pot-bellied stove and storage space for the firewood. The second room was larger and filled with those old ironwork and wooden desks that seat two children each. As my sister and I played school there, I would sometimes imagine being one of the students giving a recitation in front of the class.

Charlotte Mason believed that poetry is the highest form of literature and that children should hear poetry, memorize and recite it. She said, "All children have it in them to recite; it is an imprisoned gift waiting to be delivered... The child should speak beautiful thoughts so beautifully, with such delicate rendering of each nuance of meaning, that he becomes to the listener the interpreter of the author's thought... Consider what appreciation, sympathy, power of expression this implies... The child is led to find the just expression of the thought for himself; never is the poor teacher allowed to set a pattern — 'say this as I say it.' The ideas are kept well within the child's range, and the expression is his own." (*Home Education*, p. 223-224)

Charlotte knew a lady whose young niece could repeat any of a very long list of poems though "she had never learnt a single verse by heart in her life." After the demonstration, the method was explained to Charlotte who then used this method in her schools. Try this natural, novel way of memorizing poetry: choose a poem, read it to the child once or twice a day at odd times (during a meal or a bath); after a week of this see if the child knows the poem. (A longer poem may require more readings.)

We tend to think that in order to memorize a poem, we need to break it down and commit portions of it to memory by endless repetitions. This is what the aunt meant when she said her niece could say poems she had not learned. Miss Mason wished the child to simply listen with an open mind, unconsciously making mental images. Then the enjoyment of poetry remains.

Jean Howery has been doing memorization using this natural method with her children. Her eight-year-old son enjoys memorizing scriptures and poetry. It comes easily to him. Once when Jean was reading to Shawn, they came across a poem he had memorized in a book. He was so excited; it was like finding a lost friend! Jean posts a copy of a poem near the bathroom mirror for independent readers. She also keeps a copy of the poem on a small easel on the kitchen table so she can read it aloud while the children are eating. Instead of reading cereal boxes, let's have poetry available at mealtime.

A woman that Charlotte knew of, found that during a bed-ridden convalescence she had the ability to memorize long passages (including the whole of *Paradise Lost*) after just one reading. But as she recovered and became busy with other things, this astonishing ability vanished. "It is possible that the disengaged mind of a child is as free to take and as strong to hold beautiful images clothed in beautiful words as was that of this lady during her convalescence..." (*Home Education*, p. 226)

Wondering what poems to start with? Try to choose something appropriate to the level of your children, something enjoyable. Shorter poems would be best to start with. There are collections of poems in the library; I recently checked out *The Book of 1,000 Poems*. Karen Andreola suggests choosing a poem to go with the season, or one that correlates with a subject you are studying, or reading several poems by the same poet. Remember to train your children to not pause at the end of a line unless there is a punctuation mark. Encourage clear enunciation and expressive renditions, including body language and facial expressions.

One mother says that her children have become more attentive listeners due to narration. Memorization has now become easier for her children; she attributes this to their improved listening skills. Narration is simply putting into your own words what you have read or heard. Narration and poetry go hand in hand. Included in the Charlotte

Mason series of books are actual narrations from students. Instead of an essay, some of these narrations are in poetic form. Obviously, poetry was a major part of the curriculum to come so readily to the students. Children may also narrate poetry in prose form.

Recitation may become a new family tradition. Groups of home schooling families may wish to get together occasionally to recite poetry. Charlotte Mason felt that everyone should be able to speak effectively in public. She wished parents and educators to "train their children in the art of recitation...[because] in learning to recite you learn to speak." Our homes may not be little red schoolhouses, but we have the means of keeping some of that old-fashioned flavor of education alive by encouraging our children to recite beautifully.

A Bit of Culture

Growing up, I had little cultural exposure. No trips to museums, no concerts, no piano in the house. Money and opportunities were very limited. But I was exposed to a bit of culture through a grandmother who read aloud from an old collection of fairytales, put together a typewritten collection of several poems of interest to children, and had a small collection of classical records. But my favorite, of her bit of culture, was a massive volume of great artwork that I would browse through by the hour.

Home educators have the opportunity to give the gift of culture to our children. We have the freedom to include more humanities in our curriculum. And best of all, we can fill our own cultural cups, no matter how impoverished, as we strive to enrich our children's lives.

Charlotte Mason wrote, "Intellectual culture...this the young people must get at home, or nowhere. By this sort of culture I mean, not so much the getting of knowledge, nor even getting the power to learn, but the cultivation of the power to appreciate, to enjoy, whatever is just, true, and beautiful in thought and expression." (Vol. 5, p. 212)

Miss Mason went on to suggest that, as a family, we take time to read aloud from worthy literature. Several evenings a week, if possible, we should spend about an hour in this and other cultural pursuits. Our children should learn to read beautifully so when it is their turn to read to the family, they can read with meaning and feeling.

Charlotte loved poetry and quoted it often in her *Home Education Series*. "Poetry takes first rank as a means of intellectual culture. Goethe tells us that we ought to see a good picture, hear good music, and read some good poetry everyday." (Vol. 5 p. 224) Charlotte felt we ought to enjoy the works of one poet at a time and for a long period to become intimately acquainted with his

works. Poetry should be a part of those family evenings.

Just as we spend time with one poet, so we should spend some months with a single composer and his music. Start out with a story about the composer that the children narrate. (This step should also be done with poets and artists as you study them.) Listen to one of his pieces for a few weeks. Then listen to additional works, gradually increasing the pieces with which your family becomes well acquainted. Other anecdotes or biographies may also be read and narrated.

Keeping an art appreciation notebook is a rewarding way to help our families become intimate with art. Charlotte Mason recommended studying six works of one artist. If possible, prints of these pictures should be in our notebook along with narrations that the children tell of each picture from memory. Each picture should be studied for three or four weeks, but you need only do it once a week for five to ten minutes. The pictures should be displayed, or at least accessible during the unit on that artist. Members of the family all contribute to the same notebook, making it a true family project.

I like this quote from the Fall 1995 issue of *Parent's Review.* "Cultural education is a delight in things for their own sake... All art is an interpretation of life. Its value, therefore, is vital, not academic." — Monk Gibbons. The book, *Children of a Greater God,* by Terry Glaspey is really a book about improving our children's character through cultural mediums. In his book, Mr. Glaspey quoted George MacDonald as saying, "[In art] the fundamental idea seems to be the revelation of the true through the beautiful."

One of the great points that comes across from Charlotte Mason is that we don't need to dissect, classify, analyze, or read critical essays on the arts. We don't need to know which meter a poem employs, or what

key changes occur in a symphony, or the use of the Golden Mean in the composition of art. We parents don't need to be experts, deliver knowledgeable lectures, and generally intrude in our children's natural appreciation. All we need to do, is read or listen or look at great art and show our reverence for the inspiration and beauty of the piece.

We give our children a bit of

culture by reading aloud the best literature and poetry. We listen to good music on the radio or borrow recordings from the library. Concerts are frequent in cities and are sometimes free. Music lessons or family singing make music more personal. We visit museums and art shows — many of which are free or accept donations. We borrow or purchase books or prints of fine art. And we make art materials available to our children to create their own works of art.

We parents, and grandparents, are vital in bringing culture to children. We provide opportunities and time to enjoy and appreciate all that is "virtuous, lovely, or of good report or praiseworthy." We make acquiring a bit of culture a priority in our own lives, as well as in the lives of those we love.

Masterly Inactivity

This is a principle that Miss Mason put into practice herself with everyone with whom she had contact. She would not use her personal influence to try to manipulate others into accepting her beliefs. She wanted them to think for themselves.

A method of education "is natural; easy, yielding, unobtrusive, simple as the ways of Nature herself; yet, watchful, careful, all-pervading, all compelling... The parent who *sees his way* —that is, the exact force of method —to educate his child, will make use of every circumstance of the child's life almost without intention on his own part, so easy and spontaneous is a method of education based upon Natural Law" (Vol. 1, p. 8)

"That the child, though under supervision, should be left much to himself —both that he may go to work in his own way on the ideas he receives, and also that he may be the more open to natural influences." (p. 177)

We should have a Method of Education not a System of Education. A method is flexible, free, yielding, adaptive, natural. A system is endless rules and very rigid. The system would teach the child how to play but then he has no initiative. A wise passiveness —let children take the initiative; follow the lead of Nature. (Vol. 2, XVI)

"We are very tenacious of the dignity and individuality of our children... Do not take too much upon ourselves, but leave time and scope for the workings of Nature and of a higher Power than Nature herself." (p. 232)

"Masterly Inactivity...indicates the power to act, the desire to act, and the insight and self-restraint which forbid action... The mastery is not over ourselves only; there is also a sense of authority, which our children should be as much aware of when it is inactive as when they are doing our bidding... This element of strength is the backbone of our position... They are free under authority, which is liberty; to be free without authority is license." (Vol. 3, p. 28)

Be good-natured in your position of authority. Have confidence in self. Don't be anxious, domineering, interfering, demanding, etc. (p. 29)

"The child who is good because he must be so, loses in power of initiative more than he gains in seemly behavior. Every time a child feels that he chooses to obey of his own accord, his power of initiative is strengthened." (p. 31)

"This is the freedom which a child enjoys who has the confidence of his parents as to his comings and goings and childish doings, and who is all the time aware of their authority... He has liberty, that is, with a sense of *must* behind it to relieve him of that unrest which comes with the constant effort of decision. He is free to do as he ought, but knows quite well in his secret heart that he is not free to do that which ought not. The child who, on the contrary, grows up with no strong sense of authority behind all his actions, but who receives many exhortations to be good and obedient and what not, is aware that he may choose either good or evil, he may obey or not obey, he may tell the truth or tell a lie; and, even when he chooses aright, he does so at the cost of a great deal of nervous wear and tear. His parents have removed from him the support of their authority in the difficult choice of right-doing, and he is left alone to make that most trying of all efforts, the effort of decision... [The child] must be treated with full confidence, and must feel that right-doing is his own free choice, which his parents trust him to make; but he must also be very well aware of the deterrent force in the background, watchful to hinder him when he would do wrong." (p. 31-32)

"AN ADEQUATE DOCTRINE: The *person* of the child is sacred to us; we do not swamp his individuality in his intelligence, in his conscience, or even in his soul;...or in his physical development. The person is all these and more. We safeguard the initiative of the child and we realize that, in educational work, we must take a back seat; the teacher, even when the teacher is the parent, is not to be too much to the front." (p. 65)

TEACHING MUST NOT BE OBTRUSIVE. Avoid lectures. Personally know objects, or nature. Form relationships with actual things. We want the child to establish "relations with great minds and various minds." Don't get between child and great minds. (p. 66)

"THE ART OF STANDING ASIDE. —The art of standing aside to let a child develop the relations proper to him is the fine art of education." (p. 66-67)

"A WIDER CURRICULUM. —Give children a wide range of subjects, with the end in view of establishing in each case some one or more of the relations I have indicated. Let them learn from first-hand sources of information —really good books, the best going, on the subject they are engaged upon. Let them get at the books themselves, and do not let them be flooded with a warm diluent at the lips of their teacher. The teacher's business is to indicate, stimulate, direct and constrain to the acquirement of knowledge, but by no means to be the fountainhead and source of all knowledge. The less parents and teachers talk-in and expound their rations of knowledge and thought to the children they are educating, the better for the children... Children must be allowed to ruminate, must be left alone with their own thoughts. They will ask for help if they want it." (p. 162)

"Composition is not an adjunct but an integral part of their education in every subject... But let me again say there must be no attempt to teach composition. Our failure as teachers is that we place too little dependence on the intellectual power of our scholars, and as they are modest little souls what the teacher kindly volunteers to do for them, they feel

that they cannot do for themselves. But give them a fair field and no favor and they will describe their favorite scene from the play they have read, and much besides." (Vol. 6, p. 192)

STUDY SUGGESTIONS: Vol. 3, Chapter III; *Hints on Child Training* by Trumbull, especially chapter nine— "Letting Alone as a Means of Child Training."

Outdoor Education

Charlotte Mason had a great love for the outdoors. She thought we all should spend more time outside. Young children should spend several hours in the fresh air each day. Daily, her college students were required to spend a couple hours out in nature. This habit was carried over to their future posts where they enjoyed daily nature hikes with their students.

OUTDOOR LIFE FOR THE CHILDREN — Never be inside when you could be outside. Spend most of the first six years of life outside. Be outside with children, perhaps take a picnic to the country; keep everyone in a good mood; leave the child alone most of the time; mother may train eyes, ears, and also plant seeds of truth within child; 1-2 hours of active, vigorous play; then a short lesson or two. (Vol. 1, Part II, p. 42)

SIGHT-SEEING: after they've played for a while, mother sends them off to see who can see the most. They come back and describe the scene in detail. This fun game trains observation, expression, and increases vocabulary. If the child can't describe the thing, mother waits for the child to bring her a better description. Then they go look at it together. (p. 45)

PICTURE PAINTING —Look well; shut your eyes and see the scene in your mind. If it's not all there or blurry, look again. With eyes closed, tell all about the scene. Years later, the child will remember that view. We can have a picture gallery of these mental paintings. (p. 48)

Children should know farm crops, common plants and trees and be able to name them and describe them. (p. 51)

LIVING CREATURES —farm animals, pets, wildlife, insects. Observe animals. Let child keep his sense of wonder by not cringing when we hold some creepy-crawly. (p. 56)

Parents can spark an undying interest in nature by their attitude, as did Audubon's father. Give children a first hand knowledge of nature. Revere all life. Let kids form their own classifications for plants and animals. Press flowers and collect natural objects. (p. 59)

OUT-OF-DOOR GEOGRAPHY —Get familiar with geography naturally by getting to know rivers, forests, mountains near you. Learn to tell time by position of the sun. Learn about distance and direction. Do little exercises with a compass. Draw or sketch maps in the sand with directions labeled. (p. 72)

OUT-OF-DOOR GAMES/LESSONS —Take 10 minutes to learn 3 to 6 new French (or Spanish?) words and to review words and sentences previously learned. Let kids be noisy and active. Play active games. Continue all these outdoor activities in the winter. Walk and play in the rain, then change into dry clothes when done. (p. 80)

RED-INDIAN/SCOUTING: several people hide in ambush. Another person scouts to find the ambush then tries to sneak up on the ambushers. Do a similar thing by trying to get closer to birds and wildlife to observe them. Track a bird by its song. (p. 88-89)

STUDY SUGGESTIONS: Vol. 1, Part II

Charlotte Mason's Therapy for Moms

by Karen Rackliffe

When Moriah joined our family, it made our headcount nine. As with any change in family structure, I knew there would be adjustments to go along with the pink frills and baby hugs.

In fact, I was nervous. I knew from experience that for months following the birth of a baby, I experience depression that sometimes lasts until the baby is six to eight months old. Call it fatigue or old-fashioned cabin fever, it can be frightening.

As I pondered how to battle this feeling, I discovered Charlotte Mason's books. Her ideas of nature study and outdoor exploration lit a fire in my mind. I saw the potential power of her methods in my own situation.

Moriah was then one month old and had developed into a screamer. She was fed. She was dry. She was cuddled. And still she screamed, unless we took her outside. So outside we went. We decided to shut the books and leave the laundry and the house every day possible by one o'clock.

We went to the zoo, the park, the canyon, around the block, down to the river, anywhere outside. We filled the diaper bag with nature notebooks, field guides, paints and pencils.

Moriah learned to coo and crawl, babble and scoot in the real world. She was always happy in the car or stroller. She seemed endlessly entertained by watching the wind move through leaves or by running her hands through long grass.

And the rest of us? We learned how to pack fast and light. We learned to paint, to record observations, to wonder at wildflowers and research their diversity. We learned about birds and built a feeder. We learned about animals and trees first hand, which made the books even more interesting. We tracked animals in the snow. We exercised: hiking, running, jumping rocks, climbing, and toting the baby. We watched clouds. We learned about weather, painting in the rain, keeping sunscreen in the car, and wearing hats. We all learned to keep track of our shoes or be left behind. We narrated our adventures to Dad at night.

My seven-year-old, who was slow to speak, suddenly had things to say, words to write down. My nine-year-old made a new friend everywhere we went. My eleven-year-old wrote poems and dreamed. The four-year-old had an adventure every day. The teenagers became children again for a few hours at a time. And I...I had peace in my heart, respite from daily cares, new interest in this beautiful world, joy in my newfound hobbies of painting and birding, a deep love for this baby's unique personality, and gratitude to God for His many gifts. All this, thanks to Charlotte Mason.

Nature Study

*H*and-in-hand with outdoor life and education is nature study. Miss Mason's college students would bring back finds from their nature walks to share with her. They would often tastefully arrange some bits of moss and rocks or flowers to delight their beloved teacher.

"As soon as he is able to keep it himself, a nature-diary is a source of delight to a child. Every day's walk gives him something to enter..." (Vol. 1, p. 54-55)

"It would be well if all we persons in authority...could make up our minds that there is no sort of knowledge to be got in these early years so valuable to children as that which they live in. Let them once get touch with Nature, and a habit is formed which will be a source of delight through life. We were all meant to be naturalists, each in his degree, and it is inexcusable to live in a world so full of the marvels of plant and animal life and to care for none of these things." (p. 61)

"Reverence for *life,* as a wonderful and awful gift, which a ruthless child may destroy but never can restore, is a lesson of first importance to the child... The child who sees his mother with reverent touch lift an early snowdrop to her lips, learns a higher lesson than the 'print-books' can teach... All the 'common information' they have been gathering until then, and the habits of observation they have acquired, will form a capital groundwork for a scientific education. In the meantime, let them consider the lilies of the field and the fowls of the air." (p. 63)

"The power to classify, discriminate, distinguish between things that differ, is amongst the highest faculties of the human intellect, and no opportunity to cultivate it should be let slip; but classification got out of books, that the child does not make for himself and is not able to verify for himself, cultivates no power but that of verbal memory." (p. 64)

"The mother cannot devote herself too much to this kind of reading, not only that she may read tid-bits to her children about matters they have come across, but that she may be able to answer their queries and direct their observation. A woman...should make herself mistress of this sort of information; the children will adore her for knowing what they want to know, and who knows but she may give its bent for life to some young mind destined to do great things for the world." (p. 64-65)

"The nature notebooks...have recommended themselves pretty widely as traveling companions and life records wherein the 'find' of every season, bird or flower, fungus or moss, is sketched, and described... Certainly these notebooks do a good deal to bring science within the range of common thought and experience." (Vol. 6, p. 223)

"We are trying to open the book of nature to children by the proper key—knowledge, acquaintance by look and name, if not more, with bird and flower and tree..." (p. 328)

STUDY SUGGESTIONS: Vol. 3, p. 218-223; *Handbook of Nature Study* by L.H. Bailey

Observing the Wonderful World Around Us
by Roger and Donna Goff

INTRODUCTION

In this article, you will see how our nature study process evolved over time to include many facets. The more facets we integrated, the fuller the educational experience obtained. We are now to the point where we can integrate science, art, observation, collecting, categorizing, writing, reading, and poetry; all combined with a deeper love of nature and the world we live in. All this is done in a simple, natural manner that anyone can duplicate.

Recently, we have been introduced to the writings and philosophy of Charlotte Mason, a turn of the century British educator who strongly advocated getting out and observing nature first-hand and recording your observations. Most of the things we have learned over 16 years are contained in her philosophy. Studying her works has evoked a kindred-spirit feeling that is strong and wonderful.

So whether you are homeschooling your children and want to provide a rich multifaceted experience for them, or just desire to enrich your children's ability to appreciate nature, join us now as we explore nature together!

METHODS

Do you feel intimidated by science? Are you one of the many in our culture that has had distasteful experiences in school, turning you off to natural science? If you are homeschooling, have your friends asked the invariable "What about science" question? Many people suppose that science can only be taught and learned in the classroom, with a textbook, using expensive equipment, and taught by an accredited science teacher. Nothing could be further from the truth.

The pathway to a solid foundation in science is as close as your own front door. The methods we use are not difficult to learn or implement, and are really quite natural. These methods include: direct observation, reading of quality nature stories to our children, maintaining nature notebooks or nature journals, and the art of collecting.

The topic of nature studies requires two parts to consider. Here we will explore those experiences that have influenced us which, hopefully, will open your mind to consider new doors into the world of science through nature study. In the next part, we will share insights into the many facets and how-to's of keeping a nature notebook, and the art of proper collection techniques, integrating the skills of observation, art, writing, cataloging, identification, self-confidence, etc.

EXAMPLE

Over the years, many people and experiences have influenced me. First, there was my mother. She read to my sister and me from the time we were young, up into our teen years. These times spent together exploring new worlds through the written word were wonderful and to be cherished forever. As a mother, I have followed her example by reading to my own children. I have read living books that capture their imaginations.

When mom would go to her art class, instead of leaving me home, she took me along, gave me materials, and let me paint. From these experiences I learned the great truth that kids like to spend time with their parents, doing the things they see their parents enjoying. Therefore, if we parents want our children to enjoy the beauties of this world, they must first see our example. We must not only read for ourselves, but we must be ready and willing to read to our children. If we want them to enjoy walks, they should see us going for walks ourselves, and soon they will want us to invite them along.

My mom taught me that life should be lived with excitement and enthusiasm. Whenever my mother would leave to go do something, we would ask, "Where are you going?" She would respond, "Crazy! Wanta come along?" She knew how to enjoy life and wanted us to enjoy it, too.

STIMULATE CURIOSITY

As a young mother, about 12 years ago, living in an apartment building in Littleton, Colorado, I met a new neighbor, Vera, who had just arrived from Germany. She didn't know anyone and was soon expecting a baby in a foreign land. Having already had two boys of my own and several years of German in high school, I was able to communicate with her and help her adjust in America.

Soon after Vera had her baby, everyday she would put her in a big old-fashioned stroller and take walks. Soon she had my two boys and me (they were two and four at the time), joining her on her daily walks. The walks were always long, but the boys soon adapted. As the weeks turned into months, my sons started to notice how things along the paths changed with the seasons.

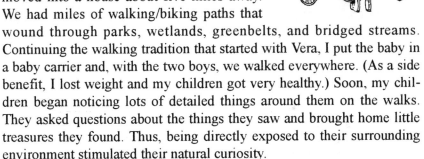

Soon after the birth of our third child, we moved into a house about five miles away. We had miles of walking/biking paths that wound through parks, wetlands, greenbelts, and bridged streams. Continuing the walking tradition that started with Vera, I put the baby in a baby carrier and, with the two boys, we walked everywhere. (As a side benefit, I lost weight and my children got very healthy.) Soon, my children began noticing lots of detailed things around them on the walks. They asked questions about the things they saw and brought home little treasures they found. Thus, being directly exposed to their surrounding environment stimulated their natural curiosity.

As we all know, curiosity is something to be satisfied, so we began the search for answers. We would search through all sorts of books together to find answers to what kind of plant or bug we had seen. The kids loved to "collect" things as they walked along. Rocks, flowers, bugs, and pinecones were their favorites. You soon learn that all the treasures of the world start looking like junk and clutter unless you organize, label, and display things properly. These skills take time, but when done right, they provide collections worth keeping. (Having your child trade or sell outdated "collections" can help your house from being buried by all their collections. Especially important if you have several kids, each with several collections!)

EXPLORE

After seven years in the Denver area, we moved to Loveland after receiving notice of a job transfer. This time our subdivision did not have any formal bike and walking paths for us to enjoy. However, after all those years of walking with our kids, the habit was strong, so we regularly walked all the streets in our subdivision. We had two more children while living there, and as soon as they could walk, they were joining the rest of us on our walks. The joy and excitement in little children's faces when they see the first daffodils of spring, or the first red rose, or the first ladybug land on their finger, are truly memories to treasure. Seeing the world anew through a child's eyes helps us as adults to really see and appreciate all the wonders that are right under our nose but are so often overlooked.

When we moved to Orem, Utah, in 1993, we again did not have any walking paths. However, it didn't take long before our children knew every nook, cranny, and flower in our neighborhood. Soon after settling in, we took the three youngest children (then age ten, four, and two) up into the mountains for a hike. We hiked clear up to the snow line before heading back. During mid-winter we have taken the entire family on the walking/bike path that goes along the Provo River. Why do we share these things? We want you to know that walking is good for all ages, any size family, no matter where you live, and in all seasons of the year. The walks need not be long. Some of our walks have been as short as once around the block. We are born naturalists, eager when young to discover and learn about our environment. So open your door and start walking today!

EDUCATION

The next area that influenced me ties into the first with my mother. I went to college and received a BA Degree in Art and Design. This, I believe, was attributable to the example of my mother. Once again, example does influence us. While I was studying art, I was introduced to the concept of the sketchbook. We were required to make sketches of the different things we were going to paint. This helped me to be a lot more observant of detail. I made sketches of still lifes, plants and flowers, outdoor scenes, geometric objects, and people.

Growing up, I had kept a personal journal. In my journal I would often write poems of things I saw or impressions or feelings I had. As I started to keep a sketchbook for my art class, I often found that adding a poem or written description alongside the sketches was a real benefit when working on an art piece. The added notation seemed to help me catch the spirit of what I was trying to capture in my sketchbook.

Good books are the last of the major categories that have influenced my evolving nature study outlook. The following are the books that have had the greatest impact:

1. *The Country Diary of an Edwardian Lady* by Edith Holden. Edith beautifully blended her nature observations with poetry, brush drawings, and anecdotes.

2. *Girl of the Limberlost* and *Freckles* by Gene Stratton-Porter. Gene's incredibly powerful and detailed description of plants, animals, and trees in the Limberlost are so accurate that many people have commented that when they first saw something in real life that she had described, they instantly recognized it.

3. John Muir's *Wild America* by the National Geographic Society (1976). His sketches and drawings of the natural splendor and beauty of Yosemite and the Redwoods in the 1800's make the soul soar.

In summary, we have discussed that the ideal way to help our children learn about and understand the natural world around them is through direct contact with nature. Kids naturally want to do the things they see parents enjoying. We can use this to channel our kids' curiosity and imagination by taking them for walks, reading to them, sketching on paper things that we see, and encouraging them through their early crude attempts.

Nature Notebooks

by Donna Gene Goff

*M*y purpose in part two is to show you how to introduce and integrate science, art, and literature into your homeschool curriculum through nature studies. In the above article, I shared the importance of establishing the habit of a daily walk with your children. I had already been walking regularly with my children for almost a decade and a half before coming in contact with the ideas of Charlotte Mason. I read a book that described many of her ideas and became intrigued by the scope of her methods. I have since acquired a six-volume set of her books, and have begun to use the ideas with my children.

In my reading of these books this past summer, I found that Charlotte Mason did many activities in conjunction with nature studies. Miss Mason taught that children should be outside for fresh air and exercise in all seasons. Children should climb trees, run, sing, and shout. She had children explore around the yard or park. Observing was called sightseeing. After sightseeing, the children would be asked to give a detailed oral narration of what they observed, this was called picture painting.

While outside, children were also taught to sing, do roundels (singing action games), bird-nesting (identifying nests and eggs), and bird-stalking (watching birds in the habitats and observing the habits). In addition, being out in the natural surroundings made it easy to teach about geography, foreign languages, scouting, compass use, distance measuring, telling time by the sky, weather forecasting, etc. Her books are filled with detailed simple outdoor activities. Miss Mason used outdoor resources well. One thing she had her students do was keeping a nature notebook. It is this aspect of her teachings that brings us to our subject—nature notebooks.

NATURE NOTEBOOKS

The concept of nature notebooks combines three traditional kinds of record keeping. The nature notebook is an outdoor science lab logbook, an artist's sketchbook, and a writer's journal all in one. The best example I have seen in print of a nature notebook is *A Country Diary of an Edwardian Lady* by Edith Holden. (I have wondered if Miss Holden was educated by one of Miss Mason's students.)

A great way to start your children on nature notebooks is to keep one yourself. I recommend a spiral bound sketchbook, 8 1/2 inches by 5 1/2 inches. This size notebook is light but has ample room for drawings and observations. Drawing can be done in pencil, ink, or watercolor. Miss Mason started children at age six and they did watercolor drawings, with their notes in ink. (For those who may be a bit afraid of drawing or teaching their kids how to draw, I would recommend an excellent book called *Drawing with Children* by Mona Brooks.) Make a title page at the beginning of your notebook. It should include your name and the date you begin. Don't be overly concerned about how your notebook looks in the beginning. The more a person practices and observes, the more accurate their drawings and book will become. When you look for things to add to your notebook, remember some things must be sketched where they are, while other items can be collected and brought home for a later sketching time.

Miss Mason did not like the idea of children killing bugs to collect them. She lived during the time when safari hunts and trophy rooms were status symbols. She respected life and taught her students to respect life also. She did not want children to develop a taste for the hunt, even with bugs and small animals. Drawing requires us to be more observant, more so than photography or hunting/collecting.

All drawings should be labeled with the common name of the plant or animal. Later when you can check a field guide, add the Latin or scientific name below the common name. Leave space on the page to add prose, quotes, or an original poem. Include observations of animal habits. Teach your children to calendar, i.e. have them include with each entry the date, time, and place of their observation. This helps us observe how things change with each of the seasons.

At the end of your notebook, make index lists. One list for animals, one for trees, and one for flowers. Each line item in a list should contain the item's common name, Latin name, and the page in the notebook where found. By checking this index before sketching, one can avoid unnecessary duplication. However, after checking the previous drawing, you may find that the current specimen adds new information or a different perspective, so you may then choose to proceed with the drawing. For instance, a live leaf compared to a dead autumn leaf or a bud and a blossom. This way we can begin to see that life has cycles. Children will be able to identify male birds and female birds (they really are different). They will be able to recognize trees in winter, without their leaves. As they look up Latin names and record them on their lists, they will start seeing how things are related to each other.

As your children become more observant of the world around them, they will also begin to recognize in great literature that other writers have seen and enjoyed the same beautiful things they are observing. They may decide to add Shakespeare's short prose on daffodils into their nature notebook along side their sketch of a daffodil, or perhaps a poem of their own creation.

Finally, another idea for a nature notebook can be focusing the entire notebook on one theme, such as "My summer in Alaska," or "A nature study of my yard," or even a "Leaf print notebook." For a leaf print notebook, you could teach your children how to press flowers and tree leaves and add them right into the notebook. Label them just like you would a drawing.

Remember, have fun enjoying the beautiful world around you, and start keeping a nature notebook today!

ℳethod and ℙhilosophy

This last study topic will attempt to sum up Charlotte Mason's method and philosophy of education. Her ideas are so profound that you may decide to go through this study guide again. Once you have actually experienced the success of this method, you will probably gain more insights your second time through.

A method of education "is natural; easy, yielding, unobtrusive, simple as the ways of Nature herself; yet, watchful, careful, all-pervading, all compelling...The parent who *sees his way* —that is, the exact force of method —to educate his child, will make use of every circumstance of the child's life almost without intention on his own part, so easy and spontaneous is a method of education based upon Natural Law." (Vol. 1, p. 8)

Work the brain in the morning then rest after a big lunch. Play outside in afternoons —this is also a time for hobbies and interests. Healthy children need: exercise, change of occupations, healthy diet, happy mealtimes, fresh air, walk outside everyday, ventilated house, sunshine, and balance in life. (p. 22)

"RÉSUMÉ OF SIX POINTS ALREADY CONSIDERED.
   (a) That the knowledge most valuable to the child is that which he gets with his own eyes and ears and fingers (under direction) in the open air.
   (b) That the claims of the schoolroom should not be allowed to encroach on the child's right to long hours daily for exercise and investigation.
   (c) That the child should be taken daily, if possible, to scenes — moor or meadow, park, common, or shore —where he may find new things to examine, and so add to his store of *real* knowledge. That the child's observation should be directed to flower or boulder, bird or tree; that, in fact, he should be employed in gathering the common information which is the basis of scientific knowledge.

(d) That play, vigorous healthful play, is, in its turn, fully as important as lessons, as regards both bodily health and brainpower.

(e) That the child, though under supervision, should be left much to himself — both that he may go to work in his own way on the ideas he receives, and also that he may be the more open to natural influences.

(f) That the happiness of the child is the condition of his progress; that his lessons should be joyous, and that occasions of friction in the schoolroom are greatly to be deprecated." (p. 177)

"A parent's chief duty is to form in his child right habits of thinking and behaving. Next duty is to nourish the child daily with loving, right, and noble ideas. The child having once received the idea will assimilate it in his own way, and work it into the fabric of his life... Nourish him with ideas which may bear fruit in his life." (Vol. 2, p. 228)

"THREE FOUNDATION PRINCIPLES. —Three principles which underlie the educational thought of the Union [P.N.E.U.], and the furtherance of which some of us have deeply at heart, are: —a) The recognition of authority as a fundamental principle, as universal and as inevitable in the moral world as is that of gravitation in the physical; b) the recognition of the physical basis of habits and of the important part which the formation of habits plays in education; c) the recognition of the vital character and inspiring power of ideas." (Vol. 3, p. 126)

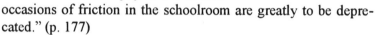

"A person is not built up from without but from within, that is, he is *living,* and all external educational appliances and activities which are intended to mold his character are decorative and not vital." (Vol. 6, p. 23)

"People are naturally divided into those who read and think and those who do not read or think; and the business of schools is to see that all their scholars shall belong to the former class; it is worth while to remember that thinking is inseparable from reading which is concerned with the content of a passage and not merely with the printed matter." (p. 31)

"If we have not proved that a child is born a person with a mind as complete and as beautiful as his beautiful little body, we can at least show that he always has all the mind he requires for his occasions; that is, that his mind is the instrument of his education and that *his education does not produce his mind.*" (p. 36)

"The work of education is greatly simplified when we realize that children, apparently all children, want to know all human knowledge; they have an appetite for what is put before them, and, knowing this, our teaching becomes buoyant with the courage of our convictions." (p. 89-90)

"The bracing atmosphere of truth and sincerity should be perceived in every school; and here again the common pursuit of knowledge by teacher and class comes to our aid and creates a current of fresh air perceptible even to the chance visitor, who sees the glow of intellectual life and moral health on the faces of teachers and children alike." (p. 97)

"We need not labor to get children to learn their lessons; that, if we would believe it, is a matter which nature takes care of. Let the lessons be of the right sort and children will learn them with delight. The call for strenuousness comes with the necessity of forming habits; but here again we are relieved. The intellectual habits of the good life form themselves in the following out of the due curriculum in the right way. As we have already urged, there is but one right way, that is, children must do the work for themselves. They must read the given pages and tell what they have read, they must perform, that is, what we may call the *act of knowing.* We are all aware, alas, what a monstrous quantity of printed matter has gone into the dustbin of our memories, because we have failed to perform that quite natural and spontaneous 'act of knowing,' as easy to a child as breathing and, if we would believe it, comparatively easy to ourselves. The reward is two-fold: no intellectual habit is so valuable as that of attention; it is a mere habit but it is also the hallmark of an educated person." (p. 99)

"The perception of the teacher is keenly interested, that his mind and their minds are working in harmony is a wonderful incentive to young scholars." (p. 172)

"It is because we have succeeded in offering Humanism under such conditions that we believe the great problem of education is at last solved. We are able to offer the Humanities (in the mother tongue) to large classes of children from illiterate homes in such a way that the teaching is received with delight and freely assimilated." (p. 235)

"Perhaps the first thing for us to do is to get a just perception of what I may call the relativity of knowledge and the mind. The mind receives knowledge, not in order that it may know, but in order that it may grow, in breadth and depth, in sound judgment and magnanimity; but in order to grow, it *must know.* " (p. 237)

"We as teachers depreciate ourselves and our office; we do not realize that in the nature of things the teacher has a prophetic power of appeal and inspiration, that his part is not the weariful task of spoonfeeding with pap-meat, but the delightful commerce of equal minds where his is the part of guide, philosopher and friend. The friction of wills which makes school work harassing ceases to a surprising degree when we deal with the children, mind to mind, through the medium of knowledge." (p. 237-238)

"Is it not then allowable to include all knowledge of which literature is a proper medium under the head of 'Humanism'? One thing at any rate we know with certainty, that no teaching, no information becomes knowledge to any of us until the individual mind has acted upon it, translated it, transformed, absorbed it, to reappear...in forms of vitality. Therefore, teaching, talk and tale, however lucid or fascinating, effect nothing until self-activity be set up; that is, self-education is the only possible education; the rest is mere veneer laid on the surface of a child's nature." (p. 240)

"Like all great ventures of life this that I propose is a venture of faith, faith in the saving power of knowledge and in the assimilative power of children. Its efficacy depends upon the fact that it is in the nature of things, that is, in the nature of knowledge and in the nature of children. Bring the two together in ways that are sanctioned by the laws of mind...and a person of character and intelligence, an admirable citizen whose own life is too full and rich for him to be an uneasy member of society." (p. 245)

"Education is part and parcel of religion and every enthusiastic teacher knows that he is obeying the precept, — 'feed my lambs' —feed with all those things which are good and wholesome for the spirit of a man; and, before all and including all, with the knowledge of God." (p. 246)

"Give children the sort of knowledge that they are fitted to assimilate, served in a literary medium, and they will pay great attention... 'The mind can know nothing except what it can express in the form of an answer to a question put by the mind to itself'... We all know the trick of it. If we want to tell the substance of a conversation, a sermon, a lecture, we 'go over it in our minds' first and the mind puts its question to itself... What next? —and lo, we have it, the whole thing complete!" (p. 256-258)

"If knowledge means so much to us, 'What is knowledge?' the reader asks. We can give only a negative answer. Knowledge is not instruction, information, scholarship, a well-stored memory. It is passed, like the light of a torch, from mind to mind, and the flame can be kindled at original minds only. Thought, we know, breeds thought; it is as a vital thought touches our minds that our ideas are vitalized, and out of our ideas comes our conduct of life." (p. 303)

STUDY SUGGESTIONS: Vol. 2, Chapters XXI and XXII; Vol. 3, Chapters VII, XIV, and XXII; Vol. 6, Chapters I and VI

Charlotte Mason's Philosophy of Education

This is a well-tested philosophy and method of education. After it had been in practice for over 30 years, Charlotte Mason wrote volume six of her series—*A Philosophy of Education*. The following is quoted from its introduction.

We want an education which shall nourish the mind while not neglecting either physical or vocational training; in short, we want a working philosophy of education. We have arrived at such a body of theory, tested and corrected by some thirty years of successful practice with thousands of children.

a) The children, not the teachers, are the responsible persons; they do the work by self-effort.

b) The teachers give sympathy and occasionally elucidate, sum up or enlarge, but the actual work is done by the scholars.

c) These read in a term one, or two, or three thousand pages, according to their age, in a large number of set books. The quantity set for each lesson allows of only a single reading; but the reading is tested by narration, or by writing on a test passage. When the terminal examination is at hand so much ground has been covered that revision is out of the question; what the children have read they know, and write on any part of it with ease and fluency, in vigorous English; they usually spell well.

d) There is no selection of studies, or of passages or of episodes, on the ground of interest. The best available book is chosen and is read through perhaps in the course of two or three years.

e) The children study many books on many subjects, but exhibit no confusion of thought, and 'howlers' are almost unknown.

f) They find that, in Bacon's phrase, "Studies serve for delight"; this delight being not in the lessons or the personality of the teacher, but purely in the 'lovely books,' 'glorious books.'

g) The books used are, whenever possible, literary in style.

h) Marks, prizes, places, rewards, punishments, praise, blame, or other inducements are not necessary to secure attention, which is voluntary, immediate and surprisingly perfect.

i) The success of the scholars in what may be called disciplinary subjects, such as Mathematics and Grammar, depends largely on the power of the teacher, though the pupils' habit of attention is of use in these too.

j) No stray lessons are given on interesting subjects; the knowledge the children get is consecutive.

"WHEREBY TEACHERS SHALL TEACH LESS AND SCHOLARS SHALL LEARN MORE."

This scheme is carried out in less time than ordinary schoolwork on the same subjects. There are no revisions, no evening lessons, no cramming or 'getting up' of subjects; therefore there is much time whether for vocational work or interests or hobbies.

All intellectual work is done in the hours of morning school, and the afternoons are given to field nature studies, drawing, handicrafts, etc. Notwithstanding these limitations the children produce a surprising amount of good intellectual work. No homework is required.

We owe it to every child to put him in communication with great minds that he may get at great thoughts; with the minds, that is, of those who have left us great works; and the only vital method of education appears to be that children should read worthy books, many worthy books.

In the nature of things then the unspoken demand of children is for a wide and very varied curriculum; it is necessary that they should have some knowledge of the wide range of interests proper to them as human beings, and for no reasons of convenience or time limitations may we curtail their proper curriculum.

THEY READ TO KNOW.

Oral teaching was to a great extent ruled out; a large number of books on many subjects were set for reading in morning school-hours; so much work was set that there was only time for a single reading; all reading was tested by a narration of the whole or a given passage, whether orally or in writing. Children working on these lines know months after that which they have read and are remarkable for their power of concentration (attention); they have little trouble with spelling or composition and become well-informed, intelligent persons.

But, it will be said, reading or hearing various books read, chapter by chapter, and then narrating or writing what has been read or some part of it, —all this is mere memory work. The value of this criticism may be readily tested; will the critic read before turning off his light a leading article from a newspaper, say, or a chapter from Boswell or Jane Austen, or one of Lamb's Essays; then, will he put himself to sleep by narrating silently what he has read. He will not be satisfied with the result but he will find that in the act of narrating every power of his mind comes into play, that points and bearing which he had not observed are brought out; that the whole is visualized and brought into relief in an extraordinary way; in fact, that scene or argument has become a part of his personal experience; he *knows,* he has assimilated what he has read. *This is not memory work.* In order to memorize, we repeat over and over a passage or a series of points or names with the aid of such clues as we can invent; we do memorize a string of facts or words, and the new possession serves its purpose for a time, but it is not assimilated, its purpose being served, we know it no more. This is memory work by means of which examinations are passed with credit. I will not try to explain (or understand!) this power to memorize; it has its subsidiary use in education, no doubt, but it must not be put in the place of the prime agent which is *attention.*

For example, to secure a conversation or an incident, we 'go over it in our minds,' that is, the mind puts itself through the process of self-questioning which I have indicated. This is what happens in the narrating of a passage read: each new consecutive incident or statement arrives because the mind asks itself. — "What next?" For this reason it is important that only one reading should be allowed; efforts to memorize weaken the power of attention, the proper activity of the mind; if it is desirable to ask questions in order to emphasize certain points, these should be asked after and not before, or during, the act of narrating.

The intellect requires a moral impulse, and we all stir our minds into action the better if there is an implied 'must' in the background; for children in class the 'must' acts through the *certainty* that they will be

required to narrate or write from what
they have read with no opportunity of
'looking up' or other devices of the
idle. Children find the act of narrating
so pleasurable in itself that urgency on
the part of the teacher is seldom necessary.

Here is a complete chain of the
educational philosophy I have endeavored to work out, which has, at
least, the merit that is successful in practice. This is, briefly, how it
works:

> —A child is a *person* with the spiritual requirements and capabili-
> ties of a person.
> —Knowledge 'nourishes' the mind as food nourishes the body.
> —A child requires knowledge as much as he requires food.
> —He is furnished with the desire for Knowledge, i.e., Curiosity:
> with the power to apprehend Knowledge, that is, attention; with
> powers of mind to deal with Knowledge that he needs as a
> human being; with power to retain and communicate such
> Knowledge; and to assimilate all that is necessary to him.
> —He requires that in most cases Knowledge be communicated to
> him in literary form; and reproduces such Knowledge touched
> by his own personality; thus his reproduction becomes original.

The natural provision for the appropriation and assimilation of
Knowledge is adequate and no stimulus is required; but some moral control is necessary to secure the act of attention; a child receives this in the
certainty that he will be required to recount what he has read.

Children have a right to the best we possess; therefore their lesson
books should be, as far as possible, our best books. They weary of talk,
and questions bore them, so that they should be allowed to use their
books for themselves; they will ask for such help as they wish for.

They require a great variety of knowledge, —about religion, the
humanities, science, art; therefore, they should have a wide curriculum,
with a definite amount of reading set for each short period of study.

The teacher affords direction, sympathy in studies, a vivifying word
here and there, help in the making of experiments, etc., as well as the
usual teaching in languages, experimental science and mathematics.

Pursued under these conditions, "Studies serve for delight," and the consciousness of daily progress is exhilarating to both teacher and children.

The mind is nourished upon ideas and absorbs facts only as these are connected with the living ideas upon which they hang. Children educated upon some such lines as these respond in a surprising way, developing capacity, character, countenance, initiative and a sense of responsibility. They are, in fact, even children, good and thoughtful citizens.

Benjamin West

by April Gardner, age 10
based on the book by Marguerite Henry

Benjamin and his family were Quakers. His father did not believe in pictures. So it was hard for Benjamin to be able to draw and paint. But his father allowed him to once in a while. But most of the time his father thought up chores for Benjamin so he would not have time for his art.

The Indians showed Benjamin how to make paint and gave him his first art lessons. They showed him how to make red out of the dirt and how to make yellow. And his mother gave him blue.

Benjamin had a friend named Jacob. Jacob could not take care of his cat so he gave it to Benjamin. Benjamin and Jacob named the kitten Grimalkin. The cat was very, very smart. Benjamin and Grimalkin were such good friends that they could not be separated for long. Benjamin used the cat's fur to make paint brushes. But Grimalkin didn't like it and his coat got very scraggly. Benjamin's family thought the cat was sick.

Then Benjamin got a package with paintings, and paints, and paintbrushes from his Uncle Phineas. One day his Uncle Phineas took him to Philadelphia. Benjamin snuck Grimalkin in his big coat so Grimalkin could go with him. His uncle saw Grimalkin's tail sticking out of Benjamin's coat but he didn't care. Benjamin got to paint a lot and people watched him. A rich merchant saw one of Benjamin's paintings. He asked him if he wanted to go to a famous painter's house with him. The famous painter asked Benjamin if he could keep his painting. So Benjamin gave him the painting.

Then Benjamin went home. He didn't hear anything about his painting for weeks. His dad got a letter asking Benjamin if he wanted to go to Philadelphia to be a student to learn about history and so that he could be a better painter.

So his parents had a big meeting. They set up all of Benjamin's paintings around the house. And the people [the Quaker community] came and saw them. They decided that Benjamin should go.

He stayed in Philadelphia for a long time and then he went to England. He became the Father of American Painting and the President of the Royal Academy of Art in England.

The Ant and the Dove

by Colton Gardner, age 9
from *The Aesop for Children*

Once a dove saw an ant fall into a river. The ant was struggling for safety. So the dove took a piece of hay and swooped down and dropped the hay right by the ant so it could float to safety.

Then a different day, the ant saw the same dove that saved the ant's life. A man was getting ready to throw a stone at the dove to kill it. Then the ant went up to his heel and stung the man. It made the man miss his aim. So the dove flew away.

The Slimy, Icky Snail

by Logan Gardner, age 8
from a story in Christian Liberty's Nature Reader

"Hello, Mr. Snail. How come you go so slow?"

"Because I have my house on my back. If you had your house on your back you would go quite as slow."

A snail has only one foot. His body is slimy. He leaves slime stuff behind him. You can follow his tracks quite easily. When he sees his prey coming, he hurries and goes in his house so they would think it is just a plain old rock.

Bach's Secret

by Colton Gardner, age 9

Bach went to his older brother's to live. He wanted to use his brother's very special music book.

But he said, "When you get older."

So one night Bach came out and copied some of it. It took him a half a year to copy the whole book.

When his brother left the house, Bach was going to play the music. So when his big brother left, he was playing it. He was having so much fun, that he didn't hear the door open when his brother came back to get his jacket. The big brother grabbed the copied book.

He said, "I said not to use my book."

Bach said, "I didn't. I copied it."

But the brother took it away and slammed the door. Then Bach had tears in his eyes. But then he realized that he had memorized the music. He played it.

King Alfred and his Army

by Colton Gardner, age 8

Once King Alfred's enemies attacked him so many times that if they attacked him one more time the enemies would have been rulers of England.

Once King Alfred dressed up like a shepherd. He wandered far. Then he came to a woodcutter's hut and begged for something to eat.

He knocked at the door begging for food. The woodcutter's wife opened the door. If King Alfred watched the cakes and made sure they didn't burn, then the wife would give him some supper. Then she went out to milk the cow.

King Alfred tried to keep his mind on the cakes but he kept thinking about the war. When the woodcutter's wife came back in, the house was full of smoke and the cakes were burned to pieces.

The woodcutter's wife yelled at King Alfred and said, "Now, none of us will have any supper because of you."

Then the woodcutter came home. He recognized the stranger by the stove. He said to his wife, "This is King Alfred."

The woodcutter's wife bowed to King Alfred's feet and said, "I'm sorry that I yelled at you."

King Alfred said, "I didn't look at the cakes. I deserved it."

The Apple and the Arrow

by Logan Gardner, age 7

Once there was a boy that was named Walter. Every single time he shot a bow and arrow, he missed. But just once he got the bull's eye with his little brother watching. His little brother was named Rudi.

Whenever his dad shot a bow and arrow, he always hit the bull's eye.

One day, Walter got tied on a tree with an apple on his head. William Tell shot the bow and arrow at the apple. He hit the apple.

Joseph Goes to Egypt
by Colton Gardner, age 8

Joseph was an innocent man. His brothers were rude. They were jealous of his beautiful coat. They threw him in a pit. They tore off his coat. They killed a goat and dipped the coat in the blood, so his dad would think animals killed him. There were some Egyptians walking by. Joseph's brothers sold him to the Egyptians.

A while after, his brothers were starving so they went to Egypt to beg for some food. They saw that their brother was a ruler. So everybody in Ur and all their people came to Egypt to live.

Valley Forge
by Logan Gardner, age 7

American soldiers were half-naked and they had bare feet. And they left blood on the trail because their bare feet were bloody and cut. They were going to Valley Forge but once in a while they stopped for a while. They stayed there all winter. They weren't very healthy. They were sick. They ate salt pork. And some of them died.

Archimedes

by April Gardner, age 11 1/2

Archimedes was the greatest scientist that ever lived. He discovered tons of stuff.

When he was working on a problem, he forgot about eating and bathing. One time, a king had a goldsmith make a crown out of pure gold. When it was done, the goldsmith delivered it to him. The king thought that maybe the gold wasn't pure gold. So he had Archimedes see if it was pure. Archimedes didn't really want to but he had to.

He didn't know how to see if it was pure gold or not. He sat there for days and days just staring at it. He forgot to bathe and he got so scraggly and dirty that finally his servants dragged him through the town with Archimedes screaming, "I have more important things to do!"

When they got to the bath place, the guy that was filling up the water was so entertained by Archimedes' screaming that he filled the tub too much —to the brim. When Archimedes got into the bathtub, some water spilt out. Then he jumped out and ran through town naked shouting, "Eureka!"

Then he filled up a little bucket of water. He put a pan underneath it to catch the water that spilled out. The king gave him a lump of gold that was exactly the same size and weight as the one he had given to the goldsmith to make the crown. Archimedes put the crown in the bucket. He measured how much water came out.

The he filled the bucket up again and put the lump of gold in. The amounts of spilled water were different. So Archimedes knew that the goldsmith had put silver in the crown. His discovery was very great.